Arnold Berleant

Living in the Landscape

Toward an Aesthetics of Environment

UNIVERSITY PRESS OF KANSAS

© 1997 by the University Press of Kansas
All rights reserved

Published by the University Press of Kansas (Lawrence, Kansas
66049), which was organized by the Kansas Board of Regents and
is operated and funded by Emporia State University, Fort Hays
State University, Kansas State University, Pittsburg State
University, the University of Kansas, and Wichita State University

Library of Congress Cataloging-in-Publication Data

Berleant, Arnold, 1932–
    Living in the landscape : toward an aesthetics of environment /
Arnold Berleant.
        p.   cm.
    Includes bibliographical references and index.
    ISBN 0-7006-0811-7 (alk. paper)
    1. Landscape assessment.   2. Environment (Aesthetics).
    3. Nature (Aesthetics).   I. Title.
    GF90.B49   1996
    304.2—dc20   96-29328

British Library Cataloguing in Publication Data is available.

Printed in the United States of America

10 9 8 7 6 5 4 3 2 1

The paper used in this publication meets the minimum
requirements of the American National Standard for Permanence
of Paper for Printed Library Materials Z39.48-1984.

To my children
and my dear friends
now and once

Contents

Acknowledgments

Many friends and colleagues have left their marks on various essays in this book. Some of them are Hilde Hein, Margaret J. King, José Reissig, Michael Shodell, Beth J. Singer, and David Sprintzen. I thank these and others who have offered suggestions. The Philosophy Study Group at the University of Connecticut at Torrington—Riva Berleant-Schiller, Sue Ellen Carrington, Beth Currie, Kenneth Fuchsman, Sarah Glaz, and Robinson Grover—discussed my earlier books and stimulated much in this one. Besides many conversations and suggestions, Peter D. Paul contributed material to Chapter One, much of which appears in our nearly completed book, *A City in the Landscape: The Environmental Aesthetics of Rochester and the Lower Genesee River Valley*. Barbara Sandrisser made valuable suggestions for several chapters. The contributions of Riva Berleant-Schiller were, as always, incalculable.

My appreciation also goes to the editors and publishers of the following journals and books for permission to reprint material that appeared in their pages in earlier versions: *The Journal of Applied Philosophy* for "The Critical Aesthetics of Disney World"; *The Structurist* for "Reflections on a Reflection: Some Thoughts on Environmental Creativity"; *The Journal of Value Inquiry* for "Aesthetics and Community"; *The Journal of Aesthetic Education* for "Education as Aesthetic Process"; Oxford University Press for "Environmental Aesthetics," from *The Encyclopedia of Aesthetics*; Rodopi for "Architecture and the Aesthetics of Continuity," from *Philosophy and Architecture*; and The State University of New York Press for "Aesthetic Function," from *Phenomenology and Natural Existence*.

Permission has been graciously granted by the National Film Board of Canada to quote a passage from Bill Mason's documentary, *Waterwalker,* and by New Directions Publishing Corporation to quote "In You the Earth," from Pablo Neurda's *The Captain's Verses.* "Anecdote of Men by the Thousand," by Wallace Stevens, was originally published in *Harmonium* by Alfred A. Knopf and Faber & Faber.

Introduction

Over the last thirty years the environmental movement has developed through different phases, deepening from a
response to specific crises to an awareness of broader issues of
public policy and human values. The public has remained engaged
throughout these changes, for the issues are real and persistent.
Many of them center on the attitudes and values about environment enacted in the political process. People are coming to insist
that decisions concerning environment weigh not only economic
and military interests but also the effects of industrial and commercial practices on the landscape, on natural resources, on society, and on human well-being in general. Moreover, the political
process is slowly shifting as the idea of polity is pressed toward
acknowledging ethnic, racial, and gender equality, toward combining international integration with local autonomy, and toward
recognizing the planetary dimensions of governmental policies.

Such major developments add complexity to the critique of environmental practices and decisions that may seem to be local or
national but often have global effects. The list of concerns is long. It
includes the many forms of pollution, the consumption of nonrenewable resources, population growth, the methods and patterns
of food production, climate change, deforestation, ozone depletion,
and declining biodiversity from the rapid extinction of species.
These developments raise ethical as well as political issues and have
led to intense philosophical questioning about how we live on this
planet as it becomes smaller and more crowded, about the consequences of our actions and practices for future generations, and
about the values that we acknowledge in our deeds as well as our
words. Environmental ethics has become one of the most active
arenas of debate and criticism.

Still other environmental interests are gaining recognition. A growing awareness of the fragility of environment and the loss of cherished landscapes has awakened many people to the transcendent values of nature. Awareness also is growing of how encounters with the natural world can breach the boundaries of our private lives and bind us more closely to the regular and enduring patterns of nature. Older traditions pushed aside by the rush to industrialize have been rediscovered, traditions that embrace a sensitivity to natural experience not mediated by the built environment, the electronic culture, and the cognitive structures of contemporary civilization. The recognition is growing, too, of the rich understanding of nature found in non-Western cultures and religions, and this has profoundly deepened the sense of the world for many whose horizons have been confined within the dominant beliefs of Western civilization.

Environmental awareness has also expanded to include the realms of imagination and art. This awareness is not only a sign of a maturing sense of environment but also a recognition that the directness and immediacy of environmental experience have aesthetic character. Yet environment has always excited aesthetic awareness. The cataclysmic events of nature evoked awe and reverence long before the idea of the sublime attempted to formulate their special aesthetic appeal. But one does not have to look for monumental acts of nature to discover aesthetic rewards, for the regularity of the natural cycles brings delight as well as the comfort of predictability. Who is insensitive to the bloom of the first snowdrops in early spring, the succession of impressionistic tones that suffuse the landscape as the leaves begin to unfold, the brilliant hues of the fall foliage, or the virgin fields of winter snow?

Many human societies, past and present, have felt humility toward nature, an attitude now lost in the denser, industrialized world. Our vulnerability to the directness of perceptual experience has been layered over with the hard veneer of what we deceptively call civilization. Yet the insensibility to such experience is both a cause and a symptom of the loss of humility, as well as a consequence of it. Perceptual sensitivity gains focus through a sense of the aesthetic dimensions of environmental experience.

Sensitivity, not just to the beauties of environment but also to the offenses and injuries to environment, is a precondition to recovering the fullness of the world.

An awareness of the aesthetic aspect of environment has begun to permeate disciplines as diverse as geography, psychology, art history, anthropology, and philosophy. Scholars and researchers are also coming to recognize the interdisciplinary nature of environmental aesthetics. Several books and collections have appeared in the last few years, and in 1994 the first of a continuing series of international conferences on environmental aesthetics was held. The recognition is growing that reflection on aesthetic values in environment is an important complement to other areas of research such as ethics, preservation, sustainable development, and resource management. This book is a philosophical inquiry into those values.

Environmental inquiry, then, has broad scope, encompassing many disciplines and interests. These are aesthetically relevant because all deal in some way with our perceptual experience of environment, and intrinsic perception is central to and dominant for aesthetics. This experience is not only sensory: perception has an aura to which memory, knowledge, and the conditioning and habits of the body all contribute. As inseparable dimensions of direct sensory experiences, these affect the range as well as the character of any environment, for even when we do not apprehend something directly in sensation, it can still affect us physically and so perceptually. It is important to add that although environmental experience is broadly inclusive, it is always particular. The conditions under which we engage bodily in a situation, including its cultural and historical character, are necessarily individual, local ones.

IN *LIVING IN THE LANDSCAPE: Toward an Aesthetics of Environment*, I carry forward ideas that I developed most recently in *Art and Engagement* and *The Aesthetics of Environment*. *Art and Engagement* ranges broadly over the arts, with architecture providing a link from the traditional fine arts to the aesthetic experience of environment. What all the arts have in common is the kind of participatory appreciation I call aesthetic engagement. *The Aesthetics of Environment* treats environment more comprehensively, ranging from general, theoretical concerns to individual descriptions and specific issues.

Crucial as the ethical environmental problems and controversies are that occupy so much public discussion, it is important to distinguish them from other environmental interests, especially aesthetic ones. Conflating ethical and aesthetic concerns obscures the different kinds of values that are part of the variegated color of environmental experience. In particular, it belittles the aesthetic and its directly perceptual character. Because most discussions of environmental problems neglect such values, it is all the more important to focus attention on them.

Furthermore, environmental problems are far more obvious than the kinds of answers they require. Failing to clarify directions and goals in the faith that they will reveal themselves of their own accord is at best self-deceiving and at worst a foil for cynical self-interest. *The Aesthetics of Environment* focused primarily on the constructive task; the treatment of particular situations, examples, and proposals suggested ways in which aesthetic concerns could enter into the design of cities, museums, space communities, and the American landscape as a whole. The book also attempted to develop a theoretical basis for the aesthetic criticism of environment, as distinct from an ethical critique, for although criticism may become eloquent in its application, it needs a philosophical foundation.

The aesthetic critique of environment has hardly begun, however. *Living in the Landscape* carries it further in both concrete and theoretical ways by its critical analysis of Disney World and its inquiry into negative aesthetics. Not only does this book enlarge the discussion of environmental values to include criticism; it also extends their range in other directions to subjects such as education, community, creativity, and the sacred. Further, the book reflects the continuing evolution of the leading ideas of the earlier volumes, for most of the essays here were written since the completion of *The Aesthetics of Environment*.

Living in the Landscape begins in chapter 1 by locating the study of environmental aesthetics in the kinds of experience, meanings, and values it characteristically involves. Chapter 2 then turns to the roots and branches of environmental aesthetics as an emerging discipline by reviewing its history, shape, and content. The focus moves next to particular issues. The analysis of Disney World in chapter 3 is an extended case study that exemplifies how aesthetic criticism can be directed to a specific environment. Chapter 4 is a comprehensive exploration of the obverse side of aesthetic value—what I call negative aesthetics—which develops a theoretical frame for negative aesthetic judgments.

But the constructive task continues to interest me, and the rest of the book deals with various ideas and issues imaginatively as well as theoretically. Starting with an expanded notion of aesthetic function in chapter 5, the remaining chapters elaborate the idea of environmental continuity, moving from the body to architecture, the educational process, and community. The final discussions of creativity and the sacred turn toward less tangible but no less real dimensions of the human environment. The chapters all join in developing the theme of continuity, which has become increasingly basic to my thinking. This book might, in fact, have been called *Natural Continuities,* for this phrase identifies the underlying concept that binds the various aspects of environment. Let me sketch out how the notion of continuity has emerged, thus providing a philosophical underpinning of the book and introducing its specific studies.

FOR MOST of its nearly 2,500 year history, philosophy in the West has sought to grasp the world by disclosing its components and structure rather than its connections and continuities. This effort began with the Milesians, who attempted to discern the basic element of which the multifarious objects that constitute the world are made—water or air or fire—and to identify the forces that underlie their interactions and transformations. Their metaphysical project quickly became more abstract and structured, and the fundamental substance of nature became, for their successors, "the boundless," "being," or number. This line of development achieved its climax in the two towering peaks of classical philosophy, Plato and Aristotle. Their contributions to this project were far more complex and abstract—idea or form for Plato and substance for Aristotle—each embedded in a sophisticated systematic order.

Yet the course of Western thought was set before they appeared by the Socratic practice of philosophical inquiry, which conceived of philosophical method as the discrimination of meanings, clarifying ideas through a dialectical process of analysis, abstraction, and conceptual refinement. Plato elaborated this insight into a complex and stable formal order underlying the kaleidoscope of experience. Aristotle developed it into a powerful and subtle array of distinctions that continue to pervade philosophical thinking. This process, which quickly turned from the analytic observation of nature to its cognitive analysis, division, and reconstruction, has marked Western philosophy's history to the present. Its development culminated in the seventeenth century, when Descartes elucidated a theme that had been continually growing in influence and that continues to dominate: the bifurcation of human and nature into mental and material substance.

Yet new intellectual forces began to grope their way out of this ultimate disposition of the problem of knowing nature by identifying its parts. It is interesting to ponder what these were, although a definitive history has yet to be written. Surely it was Kant rather than Descartes who truly founded modern philosophy by recognizing the constitutive role that human understanding has in ordering and unifying the world. Although Kant retained the classical separation of mind and experience, he strove to join them in the cognitive process, setting his faith behind the idealistic metaphysics of conceptual determination. Yet he also discovered that there were certain cases in which the presumption of an underlying analytic structure of things was inadequate. The synthetic a priori, troublesome as it was for Kantian philosophy, is more important for the insight it affirmed than for the particular mathematical and metaphysical claims Kant made for it. What the synthetic a priori recognized was that connections exist in the very nature of things, before all experience and thought.

This groping and unstable insight grew slowly in succeeding philosophical generations. The effort to establish the fundamental relatedness of things has come from different philosophical sources and taken different directions, but its enormous significance has yet to be recognized. As I see it, this development is not an extension of the main course of Western philosophy but the emergence of an entirely different grasp of the human world, one that recognizes connections rather than differences, continuity rather than separation, and the embeddedness of the human presence as knower and actor in the natural world.

As the studies in *Living in the Landscape* elaborate the environmental theme, the idea of continuity emerges as the best account of what environment is and means. Continuity, however, is not confined to environment alone; it becomes the key to a more general metaphysical understanding, much like evolution in the nineteenth century. What seems to be developing, in fact, is a new *episteme*, to use Foucault's term, an ordering principle that reshapes our understanding of the very nature of things. Yet the historical dimensions of this shift far exceed Foucault's stages. Of course, such intellectual transformations do not appear instantaneously, and I suggest that the metaphysics of continuity has been working its way forward through various phases over the past two centuries. To establish a historical argument for the idea of continuity that would succeed the classical tradition, or to elaborate a systematic metaphysics of ordinality and relation of the sort Buchler developed, is beyond the scope of an aesthetics of environment. It serves my purposes here, however, to approach the notion of continuity from the bottom up, as it were. Its exemplification and corroboration in the studies that follow provide empirical support that may be more convincing to the culture of action rather than of thought that characterizes our times.

Finally, this account intimates that a curious convergence may be developing between the diverse traditions of West and East. Although these traditions differ in content, general outlook, and history, the emerging idea of continuity in Western thought resembles leading themes of some major traditions of the East—in particular, the human integration in nature that suffuses Taoism, the reciprocity of ethical and social forces in Confucianism, and the aesthetic focus of awareness in the mindfulness of Buddhism. However, it is not the purpose of the book to extend a perspective that would bring these parallel histories to eventual convergence; it is enough to simply acknowledge that possibility before proceeding on narrower ground to pursue the idea of continuity in environment. Environmental continuity leads us to recognize that every environment of which we are a part—that is, every human environment—is a living landscape, or to offer a cognate neologism, a *humanscape*. Here, then, are ways of thinking about how we live, and how we might live, in the landscape. In illuminating our understanding, these ways of thinking may also lead us to enlarge our experience, and thus the world that is our home.

CHAPTER ONE

Aesthetics and Environment

The most enduring signs of any civilization are the artifacts it leaves behind: pyramids, statues, temples, vases, arrowheads, ax heads, petroglyphs, jewelry, earthworks, megaliths—the many material remains of the rich and complex life that constitutes human society. These objects of use, ornament, and ritual are not just fashioned with the skill that utility demands. Almost invariably they exhibit care and workmanship that go far beyond necessity: figurative and abstract designs run along borders and fill open spaces, color enlivens their surfaces, ornamental features are added to basic structures, proportions pleasing to eye and hand influence their form and dimensions. The impulse to make art leaves its mark everywhere.

Just as art emerges in the impulse to make things, human curiosity demands explanations. Myths and tales begin to offer them. These flower into the literary arts, but they also lead to more direct and deliberate attempts to understand and explain the forces that affect human life. Religion and philosophy appear. In the effort to grasp the significance of the artistic impulse and the unusual pleasures that art and the appreciation of nature evoke, people have devised explanations of the character of such satisfactions. These are formalized in the area of philosophy known as aesthetics, which concerns itself with the special values found in making and appreciating art and in the enjoyment of natural beauty. What makes such experiences important? What makes them distinctive? What distinguishes creative activity from other actions? Is there an aesthetic value that is unique, different from values of utility, from economic values, and from moral and religious values? What is the relation of the arts to nature and to the human activities they may portray? Do the arts and nature signify anything beyond themselves? These and similar questions preoccupy aesthetics.

Until recently, the literature of aesthetics gave most of its attention to the arts. The aesthetic value of nature had a minor place, often as a mere afterthought, if it was mentioned at all. There are a few notable exceptions, especially in the late eighteenth century, when aesthetics was being established as a specific area of study, and then in the nineteenth century, when Romanticism found a fitting subject in the appreciation of nature.

In the United States and increasingly in the twentieth century, the appreciation of nature was submerged in the obsessive drive toward industrialization, but this appreciation was never wholly lost. A number of distinguished naturalists worked to develop a consciousness of the importance of the natural landscape, and the National Park System was begun for the purpose of preserving the most outstanding scenic and wilderness areas of the country. In our own time, the environmental movement, energized by a history of disregard and exploitation and by growing environmental crises, has aroused public awareness. Policies and actions of industry and government that threaten the environment and endanger our well-being are increasingly being challenged. The environmental movement, by exposing the wantonly destructive practices of industry, the wasteful exploitation of nonrenewable resources, and the detrimental consequences of pollution, has become vocal in national debate and a significant influence on legislation.

These concerns—political, economic, and ethical—are critical ones, but they overlook a matter of central importance, the values for which these other interests are ultimately only the means: human well-being and the intrinsic satisfactions that are the living heart of experience. Here we must include the fulfilling relationships of friendship and love—social experience; the consciousness of belonging to history and to the universal processes of nature—metaphysical experience; and our direct engagement with the flux of sensations and meanings that mark our participation in all the activities and encounters that fill our lives—aesthetic experience. These aesthetic values—values inherent in experience—are what the arts confront, but they are found nowhere more sharply than in environment. How can we describe such experience?

Environment is more than simply our external surroundings. We are realizing with growing force that human life is intimately bound to environmental conditions and that no sharp line divides us from the environment we inhabit. As we breathe in the air around us with all its pollutants and absorb it into the bloodstream, it becomes a part of our bodies. So too with the food we eat, along with its sprays and additives. Even the clothes we wear "outside" our bodies are part of our body image, and our houses are the larger garments that express our personalities and values. The relationship is a reciprocal one, for we raise the food we eat and fashion the clothes we wear and the homes we dwell in.

Landscapes, too, bear the mark of their inhabitants. They are what geographers call "cultural landscapes," and they vary remarkably with their inhabitants. The tiny island of St. Barthélemy in the Lesser Antilles looks like the French soil its inhabitants consider it to be, just as Bermuda displays the marks of an English countryside. These landscapes are human artifacts, as much the result of skillful making as any other cultural object. At the same time as we are fashioning it, the landscape we inhabit influences our patterns of activity and, in subtle ways not well understood, colors our temperament and attitudes. This is as true of local regions in this country as it is of St. Barts and Bermuda, although the landscapes we live in easily become invisible through familiarity.

Thus the things we make make us. They both influence and are infused with our personalities, our beliefs, and our purposes. Because the artifacts of human culture include the environment in which we live as well as the objects we construct for use and delight, they acquire shape through our technology and our characteristic activities. In a sense, environment is the larger term, for it encompasses the particular objects we fashion and their physical setting, and all are inseparable from the human inhabitants. Inside and outside, consciousness and world, human being and natural processes are not pairs of opposites but aspects of the same thing: the unity of the human environment.

EXPERIENCING ENVIRONMENT

Experiencing environment, therefore, is not a matter of looking at an external landscape. In fact, it is not just a matter of looking at all. Sometimes writers attempt to associate environment with our physical surroundings and landscape with our visual perception of a scene and the ideas and attitudes through which we interpret it.[1] Yet considering human beings apart from their environment is both philosophically unfounded and scientifically false, and it leads to disastrous practical consequences. Indeed, the blame can be placed in part on the tradition, embedded in Western culture since classical Greece, that associates experience primarily with seeing and vision with the intellect. The realization is growing that both of these assumptions are false. Knowledge takes many forms, and concepts, theories, and information inhabit but one region of its varied domains. Similarly, our understanding of experience has expanded greatly to involve all the bodily senses and not just the eye. We now recognize that the conscious body does not observe the world contemplatively but participates actively in the experiential process.[2]

The distinction between *environment* and *landscape,* then, must be drawn differently to mirror this new understanding. If environment is falsely regarded as objective, and if it joins landscape in being infused with the beliefs and attitudes of those who are part of it, what then is the difference between the two? Perhaps we can say that environment is the more general term, embracing the many factors, including the human ones, that combine to form the conditions of life. Landscape, reflecting the experience of an immediate location, is more particular. It is an individual environment, its peculiar features embodying in a distinctive way the factors that constitute any environment and emphasizing the human presence as the perceptual activator of that environment. We can express this somewhat differently by saying that landscape is a lived environment. *Environment* is used here in this more general sense, but in discussing a region or in considering a specific location, it may be useful to particularize it by speaking of it as a landscape or as *the* environment or *this* environment.

This distinction bears intimately on environmental aesthetics, for the appreciation of perceptual values inherent in environment involves physical engagement. Environmental appreciation is not just looking approvingly at lovely scenery; it is driving down a winding country road, tramping along a hiking trail, paddling the course of a stream, and, in all such activities, being acutely attentive to the sounds, the smells, the feel of wind and sun, the nuances of color, shape, and pattern. It is found, too, in the deep awareness, so rare in the contemporary world, of living in a house and place to which we belong intimately both in living experience and in memory. And it arises in the kinesthetic sense of the masses and spaces that incorporate us. *Incorporate* is a good word here, for it means literally to bring our bodies in, and this engagement in a whole is what the aesthetic experience of environment involves.

At the same time, and as part of this embodied experience, we carry our knowledge, beliefs, and attitudes with us, for these participate in the process of experience and enable us to structure and interpret it. Such influences of thought and attitude also point up a crucial fact about aesthetic experience of both art and environment. It is that aesthetic valuation is not a purely personal experience, "subjective," as it is often mistakenly called, but a social one. In engaging aesthetically with environment as with art, the knowledge, beliefs, opinions, and attitudes we have are largely social, cultural, and historical in origin. These direct our attention, open or close us to what is happening, and prepare or impede our participation. Here as elsewhere, the personal is infused with the social.

There is another sense in which aesthetic experience has a social cast. An influential theory of art, the institutional theory, has recently claimed that what is considered art is determined not by any inherent property of an object or the experience associated with it, but by the institutions of the art world that accept something as art—the critics, the museums, the art public. The question for this sociological view is whether art is ultimately an arbitrary determination or whether there are distinctive characteristics of the objects and of appreciative experience that lend themselves to such an institutional designation. The extreme view holds that there are not; a more moderate one sees the institutional character of art as one element in a complex set of factors. In either case, the social factor is crucial. One can, in fact, go further by recognizing the influence of other cultural forces on aesthetic appreciation, such as artistic and aesthetic traditions, and the ways in which societies structure occasions for appreciation in museums, concert halls, and theaters. In environmental appreciation, this is done by establishing gardens, parks, trails, and campsites and by providing scenic outlooks over the landscape. Moreover, we are not pure sense perceptors, and experience is not solely sensation. Social forms and cultural patterns equip us with the means for ordering and grasping the occasions in which we are involved, through myths, theories, and other explanations. In experiencing environment aesthetically, therefore, we are engaged in a social activity, not a purely personal one, and frequently on a public occasion. Our sociality is inherent in our aesthetic experience, whether of art or of environment.

Environment—and landscape with it—is not just our physical surroundings, not only our perception of this setting, our environmental ideas and activities, or the order that society and culture give them, but all of these together. An integral whole, environment is an interrelated and interdependent union of people and place, together with their reciprocal processes. Similarly, understanding environment is not merely an additive process, a matter of putting our knowledge of separate disciplines together to arrive at a general conception, like the string of disconnected stores and businesses that constitute the ubiquitous commercial strip. Rather it requires us to recognize how the various environmental disciplines interpenetrate and inform each other, resembling the way in which sciences such as systems engineering and biological ecology pursue a holistic model. But environment is more inclusive yet, which is why we cannot break it down into elements in order to discover its aesthetic ingredient. More than any other study, the aesthetics of environment emerges as a dimension of the entire complex of objects, people, and their activities. That is why we cannot discover the aesthetic value of a landscape from a cultural resources survey of historic buildings or from an accumulation of particular amenities, such as parks or unusual natural features. *Environment* is a name for a complex, integrated whole, and its aesthetic is a dimension of that whole.

What is this qualitative experience of environment? It includes more than acute sensitivity to the delights of landscape. As noise is more insistent than music, commercial signs than paintings, or a factory than a grove of trees, the dominant environmental experience does not always assume a positive form. The aesthetics of environment must recognize the experience of landscapes that offend us in various ways: by destroying the identity and affection of place, by disrupting architectural coherence, by imposing sounds and smells that may injure as well as repel, by making our living environment hostile and even uninhabitable. Part of this criticism is aesthetic, an offense to our perceptual sensibilities and an immediate encounter with negative value. Environmental experience and criticism are the focal point of this book, and I shall have much to say about them as we proceed.

AESTHETICS IN THE LANDSCAPE

The aesthetic values of environment profoundly affect nations and cultures, as well as individuals. National groups commonly possess a mystique about their land, and this may be distorted into a possessive claim over a geographical region. Yet part of that mystique is an affection for their landscape and its beauty, and this is more innocent. Although its aesthetic values may be destroyed, they cannot be possessed. It is difficult to collect landscapes as we collect paintings, and so we must be content to visit scenic places, collecting, if you will, experiences of landscape. Some people presume to possess land, but few can presume to possess a landscape. Possession, in landscape as in love, is a manifestation of power, not appreciation. Both sacrifice intrinsic, aesthetic value to an outside purpose that is much less reputable.

Furthermore, associations with a cultural landscape are more far-reaching than such icons as the Swiss Alps, Mount Fuji, the Yangtze Gorge, or the Grand Canyon. The United States has preserved many of its natural wonders in a fine national park system, but these temples of nature are rarely a part of the ordinary landscape of daily life. Visiting them usually requires a long journey to unfamiliar regions. For most people, the lived, the living landscape is the commonplace setting of everyday life. And how we engage with the prosaic landscapes of home, work, local travel, and recreation is an important measure of the quality of our lives. How we engage *aesthetically* with our landscape is a measure of the intrinsic value of our experience.

This is aesthetics in practice, and it is reflected in the landscapes of different cultural traditions. It is impossible to visit Greece, Italy, or France without noticing the distinctive character each nationality bequeaths to the landscape. Temples that mark promontories and high places and the concept of the acropolis were integral parts of classical Greek culture.[3] The Italian genius for architecture is an inseparable part of a larger concept of human settlement in the landscape, whether on the watery margins of Venice or in the hill towns rising amid their rocky setting. In France, the fertile landscape of the cultivated garden found expression in both the lavish formal eighteenth-century gardens and the nineteenth-century redesign of Paris. In England during the late eighteenth and nineteenth centuries, the improved natural landscape of the great estate parks designed by William Kent, Humphrey Repton, and Lancelot ("Capability") Brown, influenced by the naturalistic gardens of seventeenth-century China, became conscious works of art. In all these cases, the human transformations of the landscape were guided by aesthetic concerns. Each of these traditions and practices influenced its successors, and each had an effect on how landscapes in the United States were seen, painted, and designed.

Still other cultures have contributed to an emerging concept of environmental and landscape aesthetics in the United States. Finland offers an unexpected yet valuable example of how the varied characteristics of its landscape have been integrated to maintain a balance between forest and city in a land where water is a constant presence. The Finns' deeply rooted love of northern forests on glacially shaped landforms is evident in their landscape, which has many similarities to the northern United States, from New England to Minnesota, as well as to Canada. In the metropolitan region of

Helsinki, nature venerated and preserved is a part of daily life. Built on a forested, rocky isthmus, Helsinki kept large tracts of undisturbed natural landscape as part of the city when it expanded outward to garden suburbs at the beginning of the twentieth century. Forest and estuary were as much a part of the first garden suburb of Munkkiniemi as the buildings themselves. The same cultural tradition guided the garden cities built for the expansion of Helsinki, such as Tapiola and later Itäkeskus. The germinal suburban new town in the United States, Columbia, Maryland, which was started during the 1960s, took Tapiola as its model. The concept of planned suburban settlements in forested landscapes has become a hallmark of the quality suburban centers that have softened the ethos of tract and strip development.

Thus the cultural landscape becomes a repository over time of the values that each generation attaches to a specific region. In a long-settled area, a respect for natural forms may be shown by returning small portions of the area to wilderness, but this is a limited, symbolic gesture that does not respond to the broader concerns of the settled region. Parks, which domesticate nature and make it accessible, signify a valued landscape in a different way. These traditions are shared with other northeastern and midwestern urban places and have nothing in common with the wilderness emphasis of federal land management in the arid West.

It is important to remember that these culturally transformed landscapes are of no less value than wilderness areas and are equally worth preserving. As part of the tradition that views nature as a garden, urban parks seem to contradict the modern sensibility toward wilderness. They may be substantially modified by the activities and uses of many generations, making them cultural as well as natural landscapes. The botanical garden had its origins in the nineteenth century's interest in the scientific classification of plant and animal forms, and identifying such historical values enriches appreciation. Gardens, parks, and arboretums recall an older set of landscape values. Christopher Tunnard reminds us that science is not hostile to aesthetic responses and that the separation of city from nature found in the elevation of wilderness over garden is a modern concept.[4]

The aesthetic study of a particular environment may draw from the geomorphological and historical information we have of it and from our knowledge of the cultural traditions that helped shape it, yet it is important to relate this information to perceptual experience. It is impossible to know a landscape fully by reading accounts of a region or perusing a map. Nor can we obtain such knowledge by looking at photographs, film clips, or paintings. Grasping a landscape aesthetically through such indirect means depends on the skill of the author, the artist, and the viewer or reader, and it is always difficult and partial. One contribution that the aesthetic makes to the cognition of landscape lies in recognizing the human contribution to the experience as well as to the knowledge of it. Environment does not stand separate and apart to be studied and known impartially and objectively. A landscape is like a suit of clothes, empty and meaningless apart from its wearer. Without a human presence, it possesses only possibilities. The human contribution to landscape produces knowledge by being, not only by thinking; it provides an understanding gained through action, not contemplation. Furthermore, apprehending the aesthetic value of landscape in this way not only offers cognitive gratification; it also provides a means of recognizing that value in experience and may arouse an incentive to promote it. The aesthetic experience of environment, whether formalized in traditional practices or developed into guiding principles, has profound practical import.

APPRAISING LANDSCAPE

Our environmental values are exhibited by our behavior—by what we choose to do, to preserve, and to change, and by how we select and shape our experience. Environmental appreciation can be one of the great goods of life. Hiking in the woods, strolling through a charming city neighborhood, and picnicking in a park are aesthetic pleasures that many people value. Yet appreciation may be disappointed, and as we move through the landscape, it often is. There is a negative side to aesthetic experience, and we confront this more acutely in environment than in the arts because it is more inclusive and insistent. Environmental appreciation is often thwarted, and an environment may be experienced as offensive or even harmful. And because the values we experience in a landscape are not always benign, we find ourselves asking why we are disappointed and why our search for aesthetic satisfaction is so frequently frustrated.

How are we to appraise landscapes? Normative judgments are the most difficult to justify, and landscape presents peculiar difficulties of its own. Environment is bound up with many interests—utilitarian, economic, and political, as well as aesthetic—and discussion of the value of landscapes usually centers on a narrow part of this spectrum of interests. The aesthetic is rarely included, except in special cases involving historic preservation, zoning, or the designation of a national or regional monument or park. The challenge is to achieve an equitable balance of these often competing interests through a comprehensive, holistic approach. Such an approach considers the landscape as a complex of many interdependent values and not a composite of separable, isolated interests. Aesthetic value fuses with these others to form the normative dimension of landscape. Landscapes, of course, have their individual character, affected in part by the features of the region and in part by a landscape's own unique conditions and traits. Nor is every landscape equally satisfying. At one extreme, some landscapes may bring us into deep communion with nature and spirit; at the other, landscapes may degrade and injure us. Between those poles lies the largest part of our environmental experiences. Critical judgment, then, is joined with appreciation.

Criticism in the arts is a familiar process through which we form judgments about the success or failure of a particular art object. We can apply a similar critical process to a landscape.[5] Through careful examination, we can identify the varying values of the different elements in particular landscapes. Critical discussion may enhance our appreciation and, in justifying our evaluations, lead to attempts to preserve a valued landscape, or it can precipitate efforts to change a negative one.

The changing perception of wetlands is a good example of how environmental criticism can help discover landscape values. Until recently, wetlands were devalued landscapes, considered suitable only for draining or for dump sites. Such negative attitudes, however, are culturally prescribed; they do not arise from inherent features of the landscape itself. In the United States over the last few decades, critical discussion has helped prevent the degradation of such a natural landscape by changing our judgment of the wetland from a despised landscape into an appreciated one. Another example of the influence of landscape criticism is in the appreciation of a drumlin, recognizing its value both as an attractive natural form and as a geological sign of the last ice age and not just as a source of gravel. Still another example of aesthetic value instilled through environmental criticism is found in historic preservation. Dilapidated structures once demolished as eyesores are now seen as historical and cultural resources to be restored and preserved. Some parts of our environment embody negative aesthetic values that criticism has yet to confront. How should we aesthetically appraise telephone poles and power lines, commercial strips and trailer parks, suburban malls and parking lots, and business districts deserted at dark? Environmental criticism can be a valuable tool for revealing both the positive and the negative aesthetic dimensions of the landscapes we inhabit.

Valuing an environment aesthetically, then, involves processes of both appreciation and evaluation, neither of which is merely contemplative. Earlier in this chapter I wrote of appreciating environment as an active engagement in the landscape and not simply the passive visual pleasure of a panoramic view. Although we may choose certain occasions primarily for the purpose of appreciating the out-of-doors, such as driving in the countryside to enjoy the fall colors or visiting a park to hike and swim, landscape appreciation is more pervasive and inclusive than these. We engage the landscape aesthetically as we drive to work or school, go shopping, walk the dog, or picnic in a park. Whether or not we are aware of the sounds that surround us, of the quality of the light, of the smells of the street or yard, of the interplay of space and mass, these are part of our habitat and enter into our perceptual experience. The aesthetic is thus a component of every occasion, and being conscious of its perceptual forces lies at the heart of environmental appreciation. The values in our environment expand when we enlarge our sensibility and awareness and no longer confine appreciation to special occasions.

Appreciation is a word that connotes value, yet curiously enough, this value may be economic as well as aesthetic. More surprising, these values are not unrelated. A painting appreciates in value, in an economic sense, to be sure, but this depends at some point on the aesthetic value people find in it, although both are complicated by current fashion and cultural biases. The same relationship holds in environment. A clear instance of the interrelation of aesthetic and economic values in the landscape is found in waterfront property or in homes or apartments facing a park or a square. The economic value of these places is enhanced by the aesthetic value of the location. Economic value based on physical location has declined since the time it was determined by proximity to the streetcar or bus stop, whereas the aesthetic source of economic value has increased in importance. Historic districts, which improve the aesthetic qualities of their immediate environment, increase the economic value of the district.

Conflict between aesthetic and economic values often results in the separation of individual property interests from the broader social context and public interests. Yet perception is not confined by property lines, and the value of a particular house or building depends in part on both its larger natural setting and its public location. For example, a community whose homes have increased in value because of their setting in a stream valley is destabilized if that setting is destroyed by logging on the hillsides, gravel mining on the slopes, or damming the stream. The conflict between property owners and those who exploit the surroundings for profit appears to be entirely economic, yet the economic values of the home owners are related to the aesthetic value of the location.

In recent years the aesthetic aspect of environment has begun to attract wider attention. Psychologists, planners, geographers, philosophers, environmentalists, and, indeed, the general public are increasingly recognizing the aesthetic dimension of environment. The problem, however, lies in determining and applying this value. Aesthetic value is elusive and ambiguous, and the response of environmental professionals seems to alternate between two extremes. On the one hand, there is a strong emotional recognition of landscape values, and on the other, there is an effort to develop principles and criteria for determining landscape beauty and objective mechanisms for measuring its value quantitatively.

Although both emotional adherence and measurement techniques have their place, neither provides the best guide for appraising the aesthetic value of landscape. The first relies too heavily on a personal, highly subjective, and ephemeral response to environmental beauty and does not adequately recognize the social, cultural, and historical factors that inform the aesthetic environment. The second, in an effort to achieve the kind of objectivity and precision we uncritically attribute to science, has too narrow a scope and uses weak or questionable data. Although questionnaires and photo-surrogates in landscape assessment studies may produce some useful information, it is clear that these instruments are far removed from the experience of landscape. Using untutored opinion and substituting small, still photographs for active physical engagement in a landscape can easily distort and trivialize the character and quality of such experience. Furthermore, attempts to quantify the response to landscape often do not take into account differences in people's experience and knowledge of landscapes and differences in their perceptual acuteness and skill, nor do they recognize the personal contribution everyone makes to an appreciative situation. The hard quantitative data that such studies produce offer only limited, perhaps specious evidence for any conclusions that may be drawn from them. Aristotle's advice on normative methodology is nowhere more valuable than for questions of this sort: one should not expect more precision than the nature of the subject allows.[6] Although Aristotle was referring specifically to ethical value, the point applies even more to aesthetic value. Finally, both the emotional and the quantitative methods often assume erroneously that environmental appreciation is visual in character.

Yet how else can we proceed? What can we say about the aesthetic value of environment that is neither a personal impression nor an inappropriately precise judgment? What kind of normative judgment is possible with landscape? If both the emotional and the quantitative approaches are limited and misleading, what other models might serve?

Two possibilities suggest themselves. One is the model of biology. How, for example, would one address the question, What is an osprey? One would describe the physical characteristics that enable a person to recognize an osprey and distinguish it from an eagle or a great blue heron. One would also describe its habitat and characteristic behavior. The answer would be based on carefully observed and recorded phenomena that indicate typical patterns of appearance, structure, and behavior. One would not describe an osprey's chemical characteristics or discuss the action of the calcium atoms in its skeletal structure, because these deal with different scientific questions. Function, behavior, process, context— these become central factors in understanding an osprey and the basis for judging its success as an organism.

Another model is that of art. We are allowed our opinions of specific art objects, but as Hume once explained, a competent critic draws on a special knowledge of art, the ability to draw meaningful comparisons, extensive experience, a highly developed perceptual ability, a sensitive imagination, good sense, and the ability to resist the influence of prejudices.[7] Knowledge of the history of the art, of its genres, movements, and techniques, must join with an acute and trained perceptual ability. One should expect no less from a landscape critic, and in fact, more may be needed. An environmental critic should understand the geological, cultural, and historical processes that shaped the landscape under consideration. And the perceptual abilities of a competent critic of environment cannot center around the visual sense but must involve all the sensory capacities in an active engagement with environment.

These two models complement each other. The biological contributes the sense of a complex whose elements and features are fused into an active whole. The artistic offers the contribution of a discriminating perceptual process, deeply informed by knowledge and past experience. Joined together, they suggest a basis for critical judgment in the interpenetration of landscape and experience.

Landscape criticism also requires a conceptual framework. It must develop clear categories by which to judge a landscape. Concepts such as 'offensive,' 'banal,' 'dull,' 'unfulfilled,' 'inappropriate,' 'trivializing,' 'deceptive,' and 'destructive' are useful in identifying and judging negative features of an environment. At the same time, we must recognize that we cannot rank landscapes. Normative experience is too complex. It involves the multiple dimensions of perception, imagination, memory, and knowledge that enter into our engagement with environment. This complexity makes judgment along a linear scale naive and misleading. It is impossible to rank art objects in any simple order, but judging landscapes against a yardstick is even more futile. Mechanistic tools such as quantitative formulas for evaluation require standardization, not individuality, to operate. Landscapes, however, are unique, and they need the individual consideration that we give to objects of art.[8]

At the same time, all environments exhibit common dimensions. They are spatial and temporal; they possess mass and volume; they have color, texture, and other perceptual qualities; and they function in interplay with the body. Part of the critical process is to discern the distinctive forms of these dimensions in individual landscapes. Moreover, we bring our values and principles to particular experiences of environment. Those that we share with others can often serve as a useful guide but not a definitive standard, since differences in perceptual sensitivity, knowledge, and experience give individual form to common principles and values. We must, then, develop qualitative guidelines and procedures for evaluating landscape. Philosophical aesthetics can help identify and formulate these, practical criticism can refine them, and environmental appreciation can exemplify them.

The aesthetic dimension is thus integral to environment. It is bound up with the physical, historical, and experiential aspects of an environment, and an actively participating human presence lies at the center of environmental meaning and value. In living in the landscape, then, we not only shape the environment but also establish its values. Experiencing and appraising its aesthetic value involve an appreciation and judgment of both the environment and its inhabitants. The critique of an environment is at the same time the critique of a civilization.

An Emerging Aesthetics of Environment

The natural world has long had an aesthetic attraction, but environmental aesthetics is only now emerging as a discipline in its own right, with distinctive concepts, issues, and theories. In the last two decades, scholars have begun in earnest to develop the field from scattered beginnings that predate the current environmental movement. Environmental aesthetics does not stand apart from other kinds of research; it draws from philosophy, anthropology, psychology, literary theory and criticism, cultural geography, architecture, and environmental design, as well as from the arts. It also has implications in philosophy, in particular for ontology, ethics, and the theory of art. Moreover, environmental aesthetics can contribute to governmental policy and social practice. Like environment itself, the field of environmental aesthetics extends broadly and on many levels. This chapter explores it in several directions: historically, conceptually, experientially, and practically.

HISTORY

The history of environmental aesthetics before the twentieth century is the history of the aesthetics of nature. An aesthetic interest in nature has probably been present since our hominid ancestors evolved, although physical evidence goes back only some 16,000 to 20,000 years, to the cave paintings and engravings in southwestern Europe. Curiously enough, these early manifestations of art are environmental, for the caves were not picture galleries but total environments that even today require active participation. Preliterate societies characteristically exhibit an aesthetic sensibility that is thoroughly integrated into their religious beliefs and everyday activities, giving us good reason to think that an aesthetic aspect infused people's attitudes and practices toward the natural world throughout prehistory.

Since the early history of Western civilization, not to mention the longer duration of Egyptian and Asian cultures, people have found aesthetic value in nature. Twenty-four hundred years ago, Aristotle recognized the beauty and order of nature, and a century later, Chrysippus, the Stoic, claimed that the peacock's tail is proof that beauty is a value in nature. An aesthetic sensibility infuses the didactic nature poetry of Virgil and the philosophical poetry of Lucretius; the New Testament writers extolled the lilies of the field, the charm in the bending of a stalk of grain, and the gaping of ripe figs. Nature has long been a source and inspiration for aesthetic appreciation.

Attention to the aesthetic dimensions of landscape developed gradually in Europe during succeeding centuries. As the slow but cumulative process of clearing the forests left great reaches of open land, the practice of planting trees increased, and people began to discover a sense of pleasure in woodlands. This culminated in the eighteenth century, when attitudes shifted definitively away from regarding wilderness as savage and threatening and toward viewing the forest as a domain of beauty. Indeed, the idea of the picturesque became popular in England at this time, and it was fashionable to express aesthetic delight in the charm of a rural landscape. The most influential picturesque theorists, William Gilpin, Richard Payne Knight, and Uvedale Price, were in close agreement in rejecting regularity of design and systematic order in favor of irregularity, variation, wildness, change, and decay. The picturesque, moreover, typifies the eighteenth-century aesthetic of gentlemanly contemplative observation. When viewed through the frame of a Claude glass as if it were a painting, the landscape was exclusively visual; observers saw only surfaces and ignored, for example, the condition of the picturesque rural poor.[1] Yet "by naturalizing art and aestheticizing nature, the Picturesque continually transgressed the boundary between the two, collapsing them into versions of each other,"[2] and suggesting a common mode of appreciation.

Much of the direct aesthetic attention to nature, though, lay in using it as a model for art. The imitation of nature dominated art from classical times through the eighteenth century and has continued in attenuated form into our own time. Gardens often reversed this relationship, applying artistic principles in refashioning nature. The designs of medieval and Renaissance gardens and the formal garden traditions in Italy and France reflect the same careful fashioning as the arts, and until the eighteenth century, gardens were often included among the fine arts. Other traditions in garden design, such as the Chinese and Japanese, select elements from the larger landscape, often incorporating distant views. In England during the late eighteenth and nineteenth centuries, the naturalistic landscape designs of Kent, Repton, and Brown deliberately shaped the beauty recognized in uncultivated nature and, like the Asian gardens, utilized "borrowed landscapes."

An aesthetic interest in nature signified a shift in attitude toward the environment, a change that is still taking place. The great Kantian synthesis that reconciled the human realm with the natural one was grounded in subjective purposiveness, since purpose could be found in both nature and humans, and it used the power of imagination to direct our response to nature. Yet it was the imagination of poets and essayists more than of philosophers that pursued the interest in natural beauty that began during that period. Some nineteenth-century philosophers and writers, such as Hegel, Flaubert, and Baudelaire, tilted the balance between the natural and the human to find the ideal in art rather than nature. The two achieved greater equality among the Romantics and inspired Wordsworth to particular eloquence. Ruskin's tendency to equalize the relation of the human world with the natural was a precursor of certain contemporary views. For him, nature not only is the source of visual beauty but also retains its original aesthetic value, and a great artist is one who is able to convey its reality. This connection becomes more explicit in Schelling, who united in aesthetic activity both the ideal world of art and the real world of objects.

The rationalists of this period attempted to regulate natural beauty by design, order, harmony, and, for Kant, purposiveness. During this same time, however, the idea of the sublime emerged as the correlative of beauty, designating aesthetic experience that surpasses the controls that maintain art within rational bounds. As far back as the third century, Longinus had recognized that the sublime possesses the capacity to overpower the constraints of reason and order. It induces ecstasy in the appreciator, he observed, who prances and rears like a horse, fancying himself the creator of the literary work being recited. The sublime, in fact, disrupts the balance of nature and art to make nature preeminent. During the eighteenth century, when the sublime assumed a central place in aesthetic discussion, it was not literature but the natural world that became its exemplar, for it is unbridled nature that most strikingly exceeds the constraints of order and limit. Early in that century, Addison cited one source of aesthetic pleasure in the great, the vast, and the grand, such as a boundless desert, mountain ranges, and a wide expanse of water. Kant, late in the same century, retained Burke's association between the sublime in literature and the emotion of terror and its power over the imagination, but he ascribed sublimity to nature only, not to art. It is nature's size or might that excites this response: the innumerable stars in the heavens and the sands of the seashore, or the force of a storm at sea and a torrent of falling water. Although this concept led Kant back to human reason and the moral dignity of humankind, it recognized the capacity of nature, unbounded in its size and power, to surpass the human. Nature, indeed, excites aesthetic admiration in its very excesses.

Over the past two centuries, the aesthetic appeal of environment has broadened further to incorporate architectural and interior design, on the one hand, and the city and the commercial and industrial landscape, on the other. The normative range of aesthetics has also been extended to allow for negative values: a significant part of the criticism by the environmental movement is aesthetic in character. Efforts have also been made to place environmental aesthetics on a scientific basis by environmental psychologists, cultural geographers, and others.

Nature as an inspiration for art, the aesthetics of nature, ideas of the picturesque and the sublime, and environmental aesthetics are all different, yet they can be seen as stages in a single evolutionary process. The recognition has grown, too, not only of the power, magnitude, and importance of nature but also of its fragility. This increased awareness has combined in our own century with a heightened recognition of our interdependence with nature to encourage the reinterpretation of nature as environment. Such a modification of the sense of nature has also stimulated efforts to fashion ideas that reflect nature's aesthetic dimension and to understand the human place in an aesthetics of environment. Replacing the concept of nature with that of environment is more than a shift in terminological style: it represents a stage in the transformation of our understanding.

SCOPE AND TERMINOLOGY

Perhaps here more than in most fields, the use of familiar terms in environmental aesthetics is tendentious. Words such as *nature, landscape,* and *environment* carry long associations with conventional beliefs and philosophical thought that make it difficult for environmental aesthetics to develop as a free and independent field of study. Social influences on our understanding of the natural world are powerful, and ethnic traditions incorporate a wide range of beliefs and practices concerning environment. When theories of beauty and aesthetic value are directed to environment, then, they face a multitude of meanings and practices that are even more varied and diffuse than those associated with art. In fact, the scope of the subject is even more difficult to circumscribe.

Environment is a word that has acquired many meanings. Taken narrowly in its etymological sense, it denotes the region that surrounds something (from the French *en*, in, and *viron*, circuit). Conceived most broadly, it is sometimes confused with *ecology*, which refers to the complex set of relations that bind an organism to its environment, or with *ecosystem*, which signifies those relations taken as a functional, interactive system of organisms and their environment. Most meanings of environment lie within this range and have a highly significant implication: they retain to some degree the assumption of an object and its surroundings or a self and its setting, bound together in varying degrees of intimacy but ultimately distinct and separate. This dualistic presumption has been challenged increasingly by scientific and philosophical developments in the twentieth century. Relativity physics, quantum mechanics, and operationism, together with the increasing influence of philosophical pragmatism, phenomenology, and hermeneutics, all deny the principal presupposition of our conventional terminology that organism and environment are discrete entities that can be located and defined separately. These recent developments have encouraged attempts to understand environment in ways that incorporate ideas of inclusion and continuity. The biological concept of an ecosystem is one such proposal. Another more general one is to consider environment as a unified field incorporating a complex order of animate and inanimate objects bound together in spatial and causal transactions, and whose fluid boundaries respond to geographical conditions, human activity, and other such influences.

Landscape raises similar difficulties. Geographers tend to define it in visual ways as the space of the earth's surface that extends from the viewer's eye to the horizon. A similar understanding is reflected by the common idea of a natural landscape as an expanse of scenery seen in a single view, and in the genre of landscape painting as representing such a view. Yet with landscape, too, we can identify a range of alternatives, from the panoramic landscape that easily turns an environment into a visual object, to the participatory landscape that incorporates the appreciator perceptually and relinquishes any sense of separateness. As with environment, the issue of separation from or continuity with the perceiver remains problematic.

These alternatives suggest that the heart of the problem lies in different conceptions of *nature*, the most inclusive of these terms. Perhaps we can recognize the changing meanings and implications of the alternatives more clearly here. The familiar notion of nature as everything outside the human sphere places the natural realm separate and apart. Until the early decades of the twentieth century, natural science adopted and refined this model, considering nature as an objective system of spatiotemporal objects and events that can be designated in specific and absolute terms. Related to this conception is the familiar idea of nature as that part of the world unchanged by human action, a view codified in the conventional distinction between the natural and the artificial.

As a consequence of increasingly influential developments in philosophy and theoretical physics, on the one hand, and pressing ecological issues and the conservation movement, on the other, people have begun to rethink the customary understanding of nature. Challenges have been mounted against the many practical and legal barriers that circumscribe the scope of what is regarded as part of the natural world and that attempt to restrict its effects. The difficulty, perhaps the impossibility, of locating regions on the earth that have not been affected in some significant way by human activity and the recognition that human actions have transformed the planet have led to the realization that the distinction between the natural and the artificial no longer holds. In light of what we now know about the far-reaching effects of human actions—on the atmosphere, on the oceans and seas, on the polar ice caps, on climatic patterns and geographical features—it is no longer plausible to think of nature, in any significant sense, as separate from humans. Nor, conversely, can we insulate human life from the reciprocal effects of these changes. We are all bound up in one great natural system, an ecosystem of universal proportions in which no part is immune from the events and changes in the others. The natural world is, then, incorrigibly artificial and, in the largest sense, includes human beings and human works. We can only conclude that nature has become all-embracing, either in Spinoza's sense of a total order or in Heidegger's sense of existential habitation, of dwelling poetically. This brings the issue back to aesthetics.

Environmental aesthetics encompasses these divergent ideas, and its various meanings reflect the disciplinary interests and goals of different investigators. Environmental psychologists, urban and regional planners, and other behavioral scientists commonly associate environmental aesthetics with the visual beauty of landscapes. They attempt to measure it quantitatively through studies of preferential selection and behavior, with the goal of formulating guidelines for design decisions and for governmental environmental policies. *Aesthetics* here is usually taken to mean what is visually pleasing. Factors such as coherence, complexity, legibility, mystery, and attractiveness are identified for purposes of empirical studies, which determine and measure their value based on the preferences of experimental subjects. Others, including philosophers and some social scientists, consider the quantitative bias of such empirical research to be restricted and even flawed by being conceptually naive, perceptually undiscriminating, and heavily assumptive. Some choose a qualitative orientation and identify environmental aesthetics with the beauty of objects or scenes as apprehended by a skilled viewer. Those who adopt a phenomenological approach emphasize the activity of perception, the formative contribution of the perceiver in the aesthetic experience of environment, and the fundamental reciprocity of perceiver and environment.

In its largest sense, environmental aesthetics denotes the appreciative engagement of humans as part of a total environmental complex, where the intrinsic experience of sensory qualities and immediate meanings predominates. The experience of environment as an inclusive perceptual system includes such factors as space, mass, volume, time, movement, color, light, smell, sound, tactility, kinesthesia, pattern, order, and meaning. Environmental experience here is not exclusively visual but actively involves all the sensory modalities synaesthetically, engaging the participant in intense awareness. Moreover, a normative dimension suffuses the perceptual range, and this underlies positive or negative value judgments of an environment. Environmental aesthetics thus becomes the study of environmental experience and the immediate and intrinsic value of its perceptual and cognitive dimensions. This broad and inclusive sense of the aesthetics of environment underlies the more specific discussions in the chapters that follow.

DOMAINS OF ENVIRONMENTAL AESTHETICS

In practice, we always inhabit a particular environment whose boundary is the horizon of our perceptual field. Yet distinguishing among individual environments may be more troublesome than helpful, for their boundaries may overlap or be defined differently, and the environments themselves may merge with one another. Moreover, there are different types of environment with different emphases.

Architecture, not ordinarily thought of as a form of environment, is coming to be regarded as the design of the built environment rather than of isolated physical structures. Architecture shapes both interior and exterior spaces. It crafts volumes, surfaces, and patterns of movement for various purposes—domestic, industrial, commercial, governmental, celebratory. Architectural structures occupy sites that are contiguous with other environmental configurations and are often part of an urban area. The aesthetics of the architectural environment therefore merges with that of landscape architecture, as its concerns move beyond the physical boundaries of a structure to embrace its connections to the site. Architectural aesthetics also coalesces with urban design by including relationships and groupings of multiple structures and patterns of human activity.

Landscape aesthetics concerns larger domains that are often defined visually, yet not necessarily so, as we begin to understand the aesthetic inhabitation of a landscape. At one end of the spectrum, landscape aesthetics may include landscape architecture, from foundation planting and landscaping to the design of gardens and parks as perceptual wholes. At the other end of its range, it may reach to the perceptual horizon, even extending to a geographical region grasped as a whole because of similar or complementary landforms and vegetation or because of unifying human activity. Landscape aesthetics, understood most generally, may be thought of as being synonymous with the aesthetics of environment or with the aesthetics of nature.

Urban aesthetics focuses on a special landscape, the built environment, shaped almost entirely by human direction for human purposes. However, we do not have to oppose the city aesthetically to the countryside or wilderness, which is a common tendency. The city is a particular environment, made from materials obtained or derived from the natural world and embodying the same perceptual elements as other environments, but designed and controlled by human agency. Moreover, although the city is a distinctively human environment, it is an integral part of the geography of its region, from which it usually has no sharp boundaries and with which it has a reciprocal relation.

Urban aesthetics deals with the same perceptual factors that are part of all environmental experience. And as the preeminent cultural environment, the city's social and historical dimensions are inseparable from its sensory ones. Aesthetic value here, then, is more than a matter of urban beauty; it encompasses the perceptual experience of meanings, traditions, familiarity, and contrast as well. Urban aesthetics must also include a consideration of negative aesthetic values: the obstruction or destruction of perceptual interest by noise pollution, air pollution, strident signage, utility lines, littered streets, and dull, trite, or oppressive building designs. Indeed, an aesthetic critique should be a key factor in evaluating a city's character and its success. To incorporate aesthetic considerations into urban planning is to place the city in the service of the values and goals that we associate with the full meaning of civilization.

The chapters that follow expand on these ideas, showing how both positive and negative aesthetic values emerge in different environmental domains. These settings may be architectural structures, a fully fashioned environment such as Disney World, or the less altered "natural" landscape. Because the human presence is integral to these domains, they are considered from the perspective of the participant as humanized landscapes. The scope of these human landscapes ranges from the standpoint of the body to the social situation to the community as a whole. In all these, aesthetic values make an essential contribution to the landscape's meaning and significance.

ENVIRONMENTAL APPRECIATION

The aesthetic appreciation of environment draws people from many different places to many different activities: visiting gardens and parks, hiking, camping, bicycling, canoeing, sailing, and even gliding and flying. For some it is the main appeal of certain sports, such as golf. But although environment is increasingly appreciated for its aesthetic character, there is active debate about the explanation and theory of that appreciation.

Certain complexities make it even more difficult to develop an aesthetics of environment than an aesthetics of art. For one thing, environment involves perceptual categories that are wider and more numerous than those usually recognized in the arts. No single sense dominates the situation; rather, all the modes of sensibility are involved. Sight, touch, hearing, smell, and taste are all active in environmental experience. So, too, is the proprioceptive awareness of internal muscular and visceral sensations and the kinesthetic sense of movement. Cognitive factors are often present in environmental appreciation to a degree found only occasionally in art. An awareness of geological and land-use history, for example, is very much a part of traversing an old footpath, viewing an eroded hillside, or climbing the rough heights of a morainal landscape.

Second, partly because of the range and activity of environmental perception, it is more difficult and often impossible to adopt the model of appreciation traditionally assigned to the arts. In fact, it is necessary to question the suitability of applying traditional ideas of aesthetic appreciation to environment. The usual account stresses a contemplative attitude, a receptive attention toward a special object separated from the appreciator and taken in isolation. This seems to lend itself to some environmental occasions, such as viewing a formal garden or enjoying the vista from a scenic overlook. Yet much environmental experience requires more active participation, such as strolling through a garden, hiking along a mountain trail, paddling a canoe down a flowing stream, or driving through a scenic countryside. Even when an environment does not demand physical engagement, part of its appeal lies in the magnetic forces that seem to emanate from it. One can feel the invitation of an entryway or the pull of a serpentine garden path. Even when standing still, the embrace of a sunset can draw one in. Such experiences make it difficult to accept the usual account of appreciation as disinterested contemplation, and this has led to theoretical accounts, such as pragmatic and phenomenological ones, that emphasize the active qualities of environmental experience. This book goes still farther, arguing for an aesthetic engagement that rejects the traditional separation of viewer and object in favor of their total absorption in environment. Not only do the theoretical demands of environmental aesthetics require a radical rethinking of traditional aesthetic theory; they raise doubts about the appropriateness of that tradition for the arts themselves.[3]

Redefining aesthetic appreciation requires expanding other traditional aesthetic concepts when they are applied to environment. Beauty, for example, no longer concerns the formal perfection of a prized object but becomes the pervasive aesthetic value of an environmental situation. That value is measured less by formal traits than by perceptual immediacy and intensity in enhancing the intimate bond of person and place. The sublime comes into its own as an aesthetic category here. It designates experience that is not so much in contrast to beauty as an aesthetic force that comes from the sense of being part of a perceptual matrix of overwhelming magnitude or power. Creation, often important for the theory of the arts, is transmuted into an awareness and awe of natural processes, coupled with the formative contribution of an active, participating perceiver.

IMPLICATIONS AND APPLICATIONS

Theoretical considerations and practical purposes are inseparable in environmental aesthetics, and properly so. As the landscape of daily life and the landscape of appreciation are indivisible in practice, so too are the theory of environmental aesthetics and its applications. The aesthetic dimension of environment becomes increasingly compelling as industrialization and its products irretrievably affect the land surfaces, the seas, and the atmosphere of our planetary environment. Environmental aesthetics can contribute to comparative and collaborative studies in urban and regional planning; to formulating policy for parks, forests, and wilderness preserves; and to understanding issues and establishing practices for zoning and conservation.

The scope of the aesthetics of environment therefore extends far beyond the conventional limits of the work of art as an aesthetic object created for contemplative appreciation. Any environment in which an aesthetic aspect is significant possesses aesthetic value. Any human context in which the aesthetic dimension predominates is an aesthetic environment. Policies or actions that affect the aesthetic value of an environment act to that extent, then, as arts of environment. In some contexts, such as architecture and landscape design, a sense of the aesthetic has long been cultivated; in others, such as city and regional planning, it has yet to be recognized. Although there is an awareness of the aesthetic character of interior design, architecture, and landscape architecture, it has had little theoretical articulation. Yet by focusing on our immediate, active environment, these design fields challenge the object-oriented aesthetics of traditional theory. And by integrating an aesthetic function into their practical ones, they embody the denial of the convention that separates beauty and practice into separate, uncommunicating camps.

Recognizing aesthetic values in the broader environment is a recent phenomenon. As the natural landscape is overtaken by human uses and engulfed by urban sprawl, the threat to these values has become increasingly grave and their importance more commanding. As a result, landscape assessment has developed in recent years along with the environmental movement. This attempts to identify landscapes whose beauty is a value for society as a whole and whose preservation therefore lies in the public interest, although the quantitative measures commonly adopted are limited and partial at best. The aesthetic dimension of urban design and regional planning has not yet achieved clear recognition in the United States, although in other countries it is debated intensely. In political forums and in planning circles, practical and economic considerations are virtually unchallenged as the sole determinants of policy and decisions, although a literature on urban aesthetics is beginning to appear. A theoretical consequence of environmental philosophy is that all these areas exhibit the intimate relation between the aesthetic and ethical domains. The influence of environmental conditions on health, contentment, human fulfillment, and happiness is powerful and pervasive, and the aesthetic character of those conditions is a major factor in that influence. Aesthetic values are also entering into discussions over the future of wilderness areas and other environmental resources, where economic interests involving short-term private gain and local economic benefits are pitted against long-term public values.

Recent work in environmental aesthetic theory is taking a variety of directions. One concerns the aesthetics of gardens, considered historically, cross-culturally, and in relation to the traditional arts and crafts. Another is comparative aesthetics, particularly likening Western to Japanese and other Asian traditions. Sensitive studies of the aesthetic character of specific environmental features, such as snow, rain, individual colors, and light and shadow, have been highly revealing and theoretically significant. The discussion of issues includes such topics as the comparison of nature and art, the relation between the built environment and the natural one, the history and character of landscape appreciation, and the aesthetic criticism of environment. These areas and issues will undoubtedly continue to expand and multiply as environmental aesthetics achieves greater visibility and a clearer identity.

The aesthetics of environment is a rich and varied field, and its significance is just as broad. It extends the range of traditional aesthetics to encompass the many different settings in which we participate, from rooms and buildings to streets and neighborhoods, from villages and cities to the countryside and the wilderness, from the presence of an individual to the active engagement of a social group. In all these, environment must not be construed as our material surroundings alone but rather as the sociophysical context in which we participate. The salience of different factors in an environment varies with the individual case. Sometimes physical features, such as mountains, rivers, or a great tree or rock, have predominating influence and give the situation its prevailing tone. Sometimes the social aspect predominates, as in a classroom, a party, or a sporting event. Whatever the situation, environment is always inclusive, and it encompasses a multiplicity of social, physical, and perceptual features.

The significance of environmental aesthetics is equally broad. Its study demonstrates the need to restructure aesthetic theory to accommodate the varied circumstances outside the arts in which the aesthetic emerges as an important factor. An adequate theory should be able to account equally well for the presence and character of aesthetic experience in all its occurrences, whether in art or in other domains of human culture. The aesthetics of environment is theoretically important, too, for recognizing the significance of the aesthetic in contexts where it has not normally been admitted. This means acknowledging the presence of an aesthetic factor not only in the landscape but in environments of all sorts, including human situations and social relationships. Aesthetic value is not only omnipresent in environment but universal in its scope.[4] The chapters that follow will exhibit some of that unusual breadth.

CHAPTER THREE

Deconstructing
Disney World

It might seem strange to propose an aesthetic consideration of a theme park, that artificial bloom in the garden of popular culture. The aesthetic is often considered a minority interest in the modern world, yet it offers a distinctive perspective, even on an activity that has mass appeal, and can provide insights that would otherwise remain undiscovered. Aesthetic description and interpretation can illuminate the theme park in many directions: as architecture, design, theater, landscape architecture, environment. I choose the last of these, environment.

Nominally, a theme park is a combination amusement park and world's fair, a place where people forget their cares and enjoy leisurely diversion in gardenlike surroundings. Its relaxed, secure atmosphere is a marked change from the public places we frequently inhabit, such as the workplace, the market, and the thoroughfare.[1] At the same time, theme parks are complex palaces of delight that offer an extravagant variety of multisensory activities and experiences and even claim to be educational. They are places of mass entertainment, easy to enter and enjoy, whose sounds and sights engulf us as soon as we pass through the gate. The concept of "themeing" is an environmental approach to the concept of place; taken collectively, theme parks constitute a multiplicity of environments, each playing its own tune.

Disney World collects many of these themes into one enormous "fantasia," a composite of distinctive environments—futuristic, ethnic, fantasy, adventure. It is a true anthology. In its enormous variety, Disney World might be considered a microcosm of America's cultural pluralism; on the contemporary scene it stands as the kitsch of postmodernism. Yet its meanings do not lie wholly on the surface. Disney World invites a range of interpretations that parallel its postmodern ethos, making it an endlessly fertile subject for the subtextual elaborations of deconstruction. Like some of its rides whose sights appear abruptly out of the darkness, the rich significance of Disney World's environments appears on multiple levels and in strange juxtapositions. By exploring some of its multiple facets through an aesthetic analysis, we may uncover some unusual dimensions of Disney World's character as a postmodern environment. And deconstructing some of its multiple meanings not only discloses its powerful normative message but informs a moral judgment as well.

DISNEY WORLD AS AN AESTHETIC ENVIRONMENT

Theme parks are totally constructed environments whose character is decided largely by their prominent aesthetic features. These are the perceptual dimensions through which we experience an environment directly—what we hear, see, and feel with our bodies as we move through it, and how these sensory qualities combine with our knowledge and beliefs to create a unified experiential situation.

The perceptual horizon of an environment helps define its boundaries. Disney World achieves this architecturally. Each area is stylistically coherent internally and distinctive externally. The three main divisions of Disney World—Magic Kingdom, Epcot Center, and Disney–MGM Studios—are separated physically from one another and delimited by physical barriers, each punctuated by an entrance gate. Each division, in turn, breaks up into distinct areas defined by architectural style and color. In the Magic Kingdom, for example, the rustic structures of Frontierland are brown, the modernistic buildings of Tomorrowland are pink, and the green of tropical trees and plantings supports the wilderness character of Adventureland. The location and limits of each area are clear. Dominant landmarks signal its center, and sharp shifts in the prevailing color and architecture form invisible lines that separate it from neighboring areas.

Epcot Center has two major sections, Future World and World Showcase, whose pavilions house different areas of scientific technology or distinct national enclaves. Although each of these structures stands separately, garden pathways connect them, and miniature trains, buses, boats, and a monorail assist travel from one area to another. Disney–MGM Studios also has two divisions—the studio and production section, and the various set locations and entertainment features. In all three parks, each area or building offers a distinct, individual domain of time, place, or pursuit.

The usual temporal parameters disappear as soon as one passes through the gate. Only a few events are scheduled, and reservations are easy to make at electronic stations. Clocks are difficult to find, and the functions by which one usually structures time blend into a constant present. Numerous snack bars, cafeterias, and restaurants provide food for all tastes and pocketbooks on any impulse. Clean rest rooms are everywhere. Multiple opportunities for play, purchase, entertainment, excitement, education, and rest are always within easy reach. One can even live in Disney World, since several themed hotels and resorts are located tangentially, connected by pathways and miniature trains. The stress of time and the rigidity of schedules disappear, and one floats along in a pressureless, though eventful, temporal haze.

As one enters a different domain of time, so one lives in another realm of space. The outside world is quite forgotten. Architectural intimidation, so common in industrial societies, does not exist here. No skyscrapers or overpowering structures oppress the visitor. The scale of buildings is comfortably proportionate to the body, and garden areas are all about. Despite the large numbers of people, one never feels claustrophobic. Lines do not seem excessively long. They typically follow a switchback pattern, are hidden by landscaping whenever possible, and are rendered less tedious by settings and backdrops keyed to the upcoming ride or attraction. Because nothing is very high, space is experienced as largely horizontal. Everywhere there is a sense of expansiveness, even without any large, open pedestrian plaza. One's attention is drawn instead to the many local niches and attractions. All this may account for the remarkably benign behavior of its large crowds.

Most people walk everywhere, and that sets the pace of movement. This is not burdensome, for frequent garden enclaves provide places of rest and retreat. Although Disney World casts its appeal largely to a juvenile audience, it attracts families and people of all ages. In spite of the nature and diversity of its visitors, the level of stress is remarkably low, and loud voices and fast movement are rare. The leisurely pace and serendipitous atmosphere keep one in a state of relaxed anticipation. Yes, there is canned background music, but it is qualitatively better than the canned goods at other markets and effectively blankets the ambient noise. The sound system is of high quality and unobtrusive, its volume low and its speakers hidden in the garden foliage.

THE MULTIPLE REALITIES OF DISNEY WORLD

Disney World, then, is a comfortable mix of discrete regions, styles, activities, and interests. It is interesting to speculate on what makes this mélange so successful in luring people there to spend days on end without a feeling of surfeit. The clear division into distinct areas and activities, the gentle pace, the superabundance of easy satisfactions, and an unthreatening atmosphere of fantasy all belie the stresses of ordinary life and encourage feelings of comfort and pleasure. Disney World offers the visitor multiple worlds, from the storybook fantasy of the Magic Kingdom and the technological fantasy of Future World to the idealized cultural environments of World Showcase and the fragmented three-dimensional images of the movie world at Disney–MGM Studios. Disney World is, in fact, a pop postmodern environment. With its heterogeneous profusion of brief distractions and fragmentation of attention into three-minute spots, it is a flowering of our electronic, entertainment culture.

Although this giant collection offers a seemingly endless variety, there is an underlying logic in its order as well as its intent. The multitude of worlds resolves into four kinds: fantasy, adventure, futuristic, and national cultural. The fantasy environments of Disney World are idealized re-creations that freely use every cliché in the popular imagination. The Magic Kingdom is largely a world of characters and locales from cartoons and childrens' books translated into three dimensions. Liberty Square proffers romanticized history, with colonial architecture, the Liberty Bell, and a show glorifying the presidency that uses audioanimatronic figures of every president scripted into unity through a speech by Lincoln, who is cast as host. The Haunted Mansion features a ride through dark passages, with hologram ghosts to enhance its eerie effect. Mickey's Starland is filled with the bubbly happiness of Mickey Mouse cartoons transformed into life-size physical dimensions, including Mickey's house, complete with cartoonlike furnishings. Main Street USA romanticizes the turn-of-the-century small town, although its Victorian facades of businesses and bars mask themed gift shops and refreshment stands. Fantasyland's exhibits come from children's literature and include the Mad Hatter's tea party, Cinderella's castle, and Snow White and the Seven Dwarfs. In Disney–MGM Studios there is a different kind of fantasy world, the world of the movies. One can wander among studio sets and props and enjoy the live performances of sidewalk skits and strolling musicians, lulled all the while by ambient music from famous movie sound tracks. For those interested in the methods behind the magic, there are continuous tours and demonstrations in animation and special-effects studios.

Disney World's adventure environments include Frontierland, representing the American frontier of the 1890s. Its generic stores, such as Prairie Outpost and Supply, Frontierland Trading Post, Mile Long Bar, and Frontier Mercantile, all house the omnipresent gift shops, boutiques, and refreshment stands. In Adventureland, the Swiss Family Robinson's treehouse re-creates the novel's abode, using the nautical and local materials available to the shipwrecked family, as well as a jungle cruise and a sail to Caribbean pirate strongholds and treasure rooms. Throughout the park are rides, space travel simulations, three-dimensional films, and films with 360-degree screens, offering the visitor a choice of excitement.

The futuristic environments in Disney World contain euphoric presentations of a benign, high-tech future. In Tomorrowland, Mission to Mars simulates a journey to that planet, complete with a fake emergency. Dreamflight is a flight simulation with a 360-degree screen, moving the passengers into a rotating cone of beams.

The WEDway PeopleMover sends coupled cars over an electro-magnetic track. The peripheral seating in Carousel of Progress revolves around a stationary stage where progress in domestic living, especially through electricity, is lauded.

Half of Epcot Center is given over to Future World, a collection of nine major pavilions where "space-travel" movie music fills the air. The elevators typically utilize a spaceship background scenario, and this 1970s-style futurism is the overall design theme and the refrain of the commentary.

The exhibits and language of Future World sing the ideology of endless technological progress (a song as dated as many of its exhibits have become). Except for the Communicore, each of the pavilions, with its own corporate sponsorship, develops different technological futures. In addition to the Carousel of Progress (GE), there is Spaceship Earth (AT&T), a geosphere in which a history of communication is presented. The Wonders of Life (MetLife) has exhibits on the senses, the brain, pregnancy, birth, and other health-related topics. Horizons (GE) provides a trip to diverse habitats of the future. Journey into Imagination (Kodak) features a ride through the creative process. There is a change of pace in The Land (Kraft General Foods), which has exhibits on food and agriculture and a boat trip through the history of food production that culminates in a greenhouse demonstrating horticulture for use in outer space. The Living Seas (United Technologies) is built around an enormous saltwater aquarium and has displays of the marine life cycle and the history of diving. The tendentious evolution of transportation into the automobile occupies the World of Motion (GM). The history in The Universe of Energy (Exxon) is more catholic; it includes alternatives to fossil fuels.

Cultural environments are the fourth component of Disney World. Across the central lagoon at Epcot Center is World Showcase, eleven national pavilions or ethnic enclaves. Each endeavors to convey a sense of its nation and culture through replicas of famous landmarks and indigenous architectural styles, gardens, local crafts and wares, restaurants serving national cuisine, and live performances of traditional arts. The interior of the Aztec Pyramid is a Mexican village square in the evening, with market stands, a mariachi band, and an "outdoor" restaurant, leading to a boat trip that takes the visitor through the country's historical development. Norway's village square includes the entrance to the Maelstrom Viking boat ride, which docks at a fishing village. A replica of the Temple of Heaven is the centerpiece of the China pavilion, adjoining a German square complete with a St. George fountain. The architectural history of Italy appears in its mix of columns, the Venetian campanile and Doges Palace, Florentine buildings, a classical temple, a fountain of Poseidon, and even a row of cypresses in the background. An overscale synthesis of Independence Hall and the Capitol rotunda represents the United States. Japan's Tea House snack bar is a near replica of Katsura Palace, and its pagoda is a seventh-century Nara shrine. Moorish architecture, a bazaar with regional crafts, and ethnic dance performances convey Morocco. The streets of France feature Guimet's art nouveau lampposts and the background image of the Eiffel Tower. Against the half-timber and Georgian architecture of the United Kingdom, outdoor improvisational theater exemplifies its heritage of drama. Canada features a Rocky Mountain setting with a pioneering motif. Closing each day at Epcot Center, "Illuminations," a high-tech environmental light show, music, and fireworks extravaganza over the central lagoon, draws the darkened pavilions together with laser spotlights and music from different national traditions.

Despite the overwhelming profusion of buildings and events, these many environments share certain characteristics. Most striking to the reflective visitor is the thorough planning, which extends to the seemingly spontaneous parades, skits, and other street performances. Visible and invisible controls make these environments so carefree that, despite the crowds and the ceaseless activity, the public spaces never become threatening. We are in a wonderland in which people readily suspend their usual attitude and behavior and where criticism and controversy never occur.

DISNEY WORLD AS A
POSTMODERN ENVIRONMENT

This jostling multiplicity of environments actually turns Disney World into a parody of postmodernism. The most salient feature of postmodern architecture, its imaginative combination of stylistic elements from a variety of traditional sources, here assumes the hyperbole and fluidity of cartoon time and space. Like post-modern architecture, Disney World presents history without being historical itself. Despite its content of real and imaginative histories, Disney World is, in fact, ahistorical. History is idealized and fictionalized here, its selections taken from a design book for their entertainment value. The historical replicas did not develop and age, and they show no signs of the processes of time or the wear of use. Everything is changeless, eternally new, bright, and clean. Authenticity becomes irrelevant and is replaced by satisfaction. Indeed, authenticity must be given a different definition in Disney World's postmodern sense of time: when cartoon and movie characters and events come to "life," we join them in a different order of reality, a fun-loving, carefree world.

Like so many of the contemporary arts, Disney World is explicitly and intrinsically self-referential, simultaneously referring to itself and its methods as it is presenting them. Visitors continuously move in and out of both modes, concurrently participating in and learning about them. Some "informational" exhibits are pure fiction, from Mickey Mouse's bed to a tour of the technological future—fantasy about fantasy. Disney World is also culturally self-referential. It provides visitors with a tour of America's beliefs about itself and corporate beliefs about technology. Even more, it embodies those beliefs.

Like postmodern architecture, Disney World combines disparate styles with a rich complex of allusions and references and presents them as entertainment. And like postmodern architecture, its order does not lie entirely in its forms but in its meanings and interpretations. Lyotard has argued that the mark of the postmodern lies in putting forward "the unpresentable in presentation itself. . . . [It] searches for new presentations, not in order to enjoy them but in order to impart a stronger sense of the unpresentable."[2] Disney World epitomizes this conception of the postmodern, for behind its plethora of presentations lie meanings and beliefs that cannot be shown directly. There could be no more apt subject for interpretation than this, for athough Disney World offers rich material, its interpretations are multiple and often incompatible, a cognitive analogue of the eclecticism of postmodernism. Yet the very fact that they form an inconclusive order makes Disney World an ideal subject for deconstructive analysis.

DISNEY WORLD'S MULTIPLE MEANINGS

Although interpretations multiply easily, they seem to be either descriptive or critical. Of the former, the most obvious is to see Disney World as an entertainment park where visitors are encouraged to be carefree and spontaneous. People can be guided by impulse alone, without fear of unhappy consequences, for fantasy is the overall motif and every outcome is positive. This is a world of happy make-believe, a place where ordinary limits do not apply and one can do anything. As an entertainment park, Disney World succeeds admirably. It is an enormously large and successful business that has made itself into an institution of American culture with a wide and devoted following and has become a major destination for foreign visitors as well.[3]

One can also describe Disney World as an educational institution, and many of its attractions make that appeal: the activities and exhibits in Future World cover a wide range of scientific and technological areas, World Showcase is a three-dimensional travelogue, Disney–MGM Studios offers tours of animation and movie sets and studios, and Liberty Square in Magic Kingdom provides visitors with lessons in American history.

Yet behind its joyful surface lies a highly complex and intricately planned operation, for Disney World is a model of high-tech planning and population control. Everything has been thought of to ease and please its large crowds of visitors. Nothing is allowed to tarnish its brilliant image of cleanliness and order, and no trash is ever in sight.[4] An elaborate network of controls regulates all events and activities, and in a supreme gesture of self-referentiality, there is even a tour of the control center. But all this virtuoso technology and manifestly wholesome entertainment and instruction conceal a deep subconscious (metaphorically speaking) that, like its Freudian analogue, is nine-tenths submerged. As a cultural symbol, Disney World evinces subtle penetration. Behind its environment of glittering surfaces—its "wilderness of images," to use a phrase of T. S. Eliot—hide disturbing meanings. In numerous ways the park both illustrates and epitomizes the kinds of thought and practice that characterize the industrial-commercial culture of our time. One wonders how many visitors note the pervasive identification of the corporate sponsors of the giant pavilions that display and laud technology with technology itself and the kind of life it makes possible—a life that is associated with consumption. Disney World, in fact, both exemplifies and purveys the culture of consumption. It is easy, convenient, and painless to spend money here, for this is the land of consumerism. The fact that admission to the park provides entry into every building and attraction fosters a sense of free entertainment that easily encompasses the kiosks and shops that stand at every turn, and purchasing Disney Dollars, the park's scrip, encourages a sense of monetary make-believe.

Disney World is actually a soft-sell environment. Everything here seems designed for ease and pleasure, but subtle controls extend in every direction, leading to the complete manipulation of its visitors, although with disarming gentleness. In fact, Disney World stands, perhaps more than anything else, as a monument to consumer culture. Everything is converted into matter for consumption: national and ethnic traditions, science, technology, education.[5] Even the family is transformed into a unit of consumption. The history of science, of technology, and of nations is just another commodity that can be fashioned to meet the requirements of the situation and sold to the public. Moreover, the theme park actually creates history by influencing our beliefs about the past.[6] Entertainment has become big business, and the business of Disney World is entertainment: its product is pleasure, and its production is consumption. Eco considers such a place "at once absolutely realistic and absolutely fantastic. . . . Facades [are] presented to us as toy houses and invite us to enter them, but their interior is always a disguised supermarket, where you buy obsessively believing you are still playing." It is what Morawski has called a "consumerist fairyland. No codes and no norms deserve any serious attention as they cancel each other."[7] Spectacles produce excitement and a pleasant confusion, while their hidden messages, buried in the casual occurrences of mass culture, effectively take over.

What we have here is a new colonialism, a corporate colonialism over the consumer and a cultural colonialism of the high-tech nations over the Third World. The culture of consumption has appropriated the past, ethnic practices, and even science, all in the name of corporate interests, especially those that designed and operate nearly all the major pavilions in Future World. The social consequences are alarming, for despite beneficent, indulgent appearances, Disney World is in practice a totalitarian environment. One encounters no scowling face, no disagreement, no dissent, no differences, and no alternatives to the omnipresent good nature and good cheer. The Disney Corporation has strict hiring guidelines. Disney World hires only about one of every ten individuals interviewed. EuroDisneyland, outside of Paris, created a good deal of animosity by requiring its employees to display smiling faces, a custom more American than European. The fact that everything is planned so successfully means that everything is controlled, and controlled in the interests of a single optimistic message: the naive, obsolescent, modernist faith in endless progress through technology. Faith in science is never questioned; there is little awareness of the environmental problems caused by modern technology and no acknowledgement of alternative lifestyles or non-Western cultural or religious traditions.

Disney World, moreover, is no aberrant development. Disney parks are models for theme parks everywhere, and the model has even been extended to entire nations: Mexico as the Third World theme park for Americans, rural England as a theme park for escaping urban dwellers, Britain as a giant rain theme park, and the United States as a theme park for visiting Europeans.[8] To turn the world into a collection of theme parks, a future that some fear, is to conquer the very planet, using the smile as the ultimate weapon to subdue a mass population with good humor.

This is an environment, then, in which nothing is as it appears to be. Spectacular in scale and brilliant in execution, Disney World is a masterpiece of falsification.[9] Not only does Disney World run its subject matter past a distorting mirror; it actually contains *levels* of falseness. Even when something is itself authentic, its context renders it false. The architectural designs in World Showcase, for example, are accurate replicas of indigenous architectural styles; yet they are merely surfaces, what we might call "authentic facades." In back of each stands another tourist shop, a snack bar, or nothing at all. What is authenticity in such a setting? Is there such a thing as authenticity anymore?[10]

Other purposes hide behind everything. Disney World represents itself as the full flowering of the modernist ethos, with its confidence in a future guided by scientific imagination toward a technological utopia. But there is a vivid contrast between the use of that technology and the kind of experience visitors have. As we are pleasantly lulled into accepting the modernist ideology of Disney World, we are subjected to a level of exploitation that is virtuosic in its sophistication and insidious in its effects: the total co-optation of our beliefs and purposes and their ultimate absorption into the credit-card culture of consumption. Yet the juxtaposition of futuristic visions with historical and fictional experiences actually contradicts and subverts a key modernist element, the idea of steady, limitless scientific progress. Unidirectional time is abandoned for a timeless realm in which everything is constantly available and the future lies before us in eternal beneficence. There is no acknowledgment that technology has consequences and that many of the our planet's present problems—from acid rain and the depletion of the ozone layer to overpopulation, nuclear waste, and modern warfare—are the largely unplanned or unwanted results of scientific and industrial technology. And history, its hard pain painted over by a blandly sentimental romanticism, is transmuted into a flowing pageant.

Even more, the universal scope of the theme park undermines our grasp of reality. There are the multiple realities of fiction, fantasy, science, geography, history, and nationality, each with its own special claim. The distortion of their content, the blurring of distinctions among them, the deliberate confusion of their modes, and the omission of everyday economic reality ingeniously exploits the very institutions Disney World purportedly honors: children, by turning the world into a cartoon;[11] the family, by promoting social stereotypes and identifying the family with a lifestyle of consumption; ethnic traditions, by transforming them into consumable curiosities and collectibles instead of genuine practices integral to their cultures; science, by portraying it as inevitably successful and invariably benevolent; and technology, by ascribing to it a limitless capacity for improving life by inventing consumables that are always desirable.

These different realities form a heterogeneous mass, and their order is uncertain. The national enclaves of World Showcase, for instance, offer ethnic realities within the reality of Epcot Center, within the reality of Disney World, within the reality of themed hotels and resorts, within the reality of the nearby city of Orlando. Do any of these realities predominate? One might be tempted to say the "outer world" of Orlando. Yet we are hardly aware of Orlando at all, and most visitors encounter the city only from the superhighway or the airport. Furthermore, the immediacy of one's present location is inevitably the most forceful, making it constantly unclear which end is up as we move from one place to another within Disney World. This is true not only inside the theme park but outside as well. We carry such confusion away with us, just as we whistle a tune after the show is over or have uneasy dreams after watching a horror movie. Disney–MGM Studios further epitomizes this jumbled juxtaposition of worlds. Its animation studios and movie sets show how film reality is fabricated out of fragments, and the park itself encourages a breakdown of the difference between the movie illusion and actual places and events. Things are equally real and equally hollow. Is there a cultural schizophrenia at work here? This disintegration of reality structure is what Marin has called "a degenerate utopia . . . at once absolutely realistic and absolutely fantastic."[12]

Moreover, most of Disney World's multiple meanings, convincing yet not always compatible, are not delivered directly but gain force precisely through their indirection. Perhaps they are not presented immediately because they cannot be. This is Disney World's postmodernism; in Lyotard's sense, its presentation of the unpresentable. What are the hidden meanings, the subliminal forces at work here? Do we begin to discover them as we peel off the smiles? Lyotard claims that "modern aesthetics is an aesthetic of the sublime, though a nostalgic one. It allows the unpresentable to be put forward only as the missing contents; but the form, because of its recognizable consistency, continues to offer to the reader or viewer matter for solace and pleasure."[13] By presenting the unpresentable on a magnitude hitherto inconceivable and perhaps beyond rational comprehension, Disney World represents the sublime in this postmodern age: the theme park is at the same time the sublimation of commercial culture and the desublimation of the sublime. Disney World has become, in fact, our monument to the sublime, its most salient expression at the culmination of the twentieth century. Can magnitude without elevation truly attain the sublime?

THE NORMATIVE SIGNIFICANCE
OF DISNEY WORLD

I originally intended to end this chapter with an inconclusiveness appropriate to the topic. Yet deconstructing Disney World shows that the dilemma of multiple, incompatible interpretations and the impossibility of resolving them does not obliterate normative judgment. On the contrary, this discussion stands as an argument against moral indecisiveness, for normative judgment is built into the very pursuit of understanding, and this last critique embodies a powerful moral condemnation. It is true that one can see Disney World as both a fairyland for family entertainment and an enormously complex work of popular art. Surely these are its positive contributions to popular culture. But my analysis reveals that it is also a sophisticated and comprehensive subversion of personal motives, social institutions, and public values by corporate interests. Disney World stands as a megamonument to the commodification of culture. Can we determine which values in this heterogeneous mix are preeminent? Can a deconstructive analysis carry us beyond the coexistence of multiple, mutually incompatible interpretations to a moral conclusion?

The case for Disney World is obvious. In its favor stands the mass audience of the theme park. For its avid followers, regular visits are a high point of personal and family life, and they happily spend vast sums for what they perceive to be full value. Who could quarrel with family fun and healthy popular art? Yet the positive case casts many shadows. Against the elaborate serendipity of Disney World are the witnesses to the simple, unencumbered life, from the ancient Stoics to E. F. Schumacher, Scott Nearing, and the contemporary Western rediscoverers of Buddhism. To find the universe in one's backyard, as Thoreau once urged, suggests an economy directed not toward the consumption of luxuries but toward enlightenment, the cultivation of aesthetic sensibility, and a deepening of moral experience that leads us to recognize the ultimacy of life and the omnipresence of the sacred.

More compelling than this alternative, however, is the unsettling picture that presents itself when we look closely at what the theme park is and what it does. As we begin to detect the falseness and manipulation that underlie its pleasant gloss, we come to condemn its empty pleasures as soporific and exploitative. The Socratic tradition that forsakes satisfaction for understanding is a perennially sobering influence in matters such as this. Although we cannot appeal to a simple hierarchy of values, we do have a clear choice between the dissatisfactions of a Socrates and the satisfactions of a fool, to recall Mill. Here, the determination of value comes from having experienced both.[14] Once we recognize the motives and interests that underlie the theme park, can we ever again find satisfaction in its joyful surfaces?

What we approach through postmodernism is a sense of things that has been emerging slowly throughout the long and difficult century we are now concluding: the realization that the tradition of clear resolutions and final certainties distorts the facts of irresolvable difference, limited understanding, and a residual pluralism of truths and values. Dewey's recognition that "the quest for certainty" is misdirected helped inaugurate a different sense of knowledge, one governed not by the goal of complete, permanent, and univocal truth but by truths in the making—provisional, multiple nodes in a constantly altering web of knowledge affected by changing conditions, needs, and activities.[15] Yet realizing this does not abandon us to intellectual fragmentation and cognitive chaos. It calls for a conceptual landscape that is vastly different from the modernist ideal of an unequivocal order revealed by "the light of reason." We need something akin to what Merleau-Ponty called "the good dialectic," which is "capable of differentiating and of integrating into one sole universe double or even multiple meanings . . . because it envisages without restriction the plurality of the relationships and what has been called ambiguity."[16]

This means admitting value, too, into an enlarged cognitive realm. Values cannot be relegated to the shadowy region of the emotive, as the positivists would have it. We have come to realize that the normative pervades all experience, cognitive as much as any other. No human activity, scientific or artistic, can breathe air that is value neutral. Value suffuses the human presence so that whatever we touch has a normative dimension. That is why an aesthetic analysis of Disney World that began with an attempt at pure description ends with moral judgment. This does not create an unwelcome complication in the knowledge process; it recognizes that another facet on the complex jewel of human understanding has been glowing all along. We find ourselves returning, in this humanized landscape of understanding, to the insight of our classical forebears that truth and value are inseparable. But we must couple this with the recognition by contemporary science and philosophy that these are invariably contextual and contingent.

Such an approach offers a direction, at the close of the postmodern age, that may rescue us from the morass into which an overly simple epistemology has sunk us. It suggests that multiple interpretations do not all have equal weight, that postmodernism requires deconstruction, and that its deconstruction leads to a conclusion somewhat less destructive than indefiniteness and less autocratic than "Truth." By showing how realities are created and subverted, this aesthetic analysis of Disney's worlds confronts us with the pervasiveness of the normative and the inseparability of the moral and the aesthetic. The challenge of our time is to reform knowledge and value in a way that is pluralistic and open-ended yet provides the basis for both decision and action. Such a restructuring is an inevitable consequence of the inadequacies of the old millennium and the necessary precondition for the foundation of a new.

CHAPTER FOUR

The Human Touch and the Beauty of Nature

BEAUTY IN NATURE

Ruskin notes in one of his observations about nature that "the clouds, not being much liable to man's interference, are always beautifully arranged."[1] It is a revealing comment, for the sky is surely one of the most striking natural wonders. What is especially fascinating about the sky are the endless configurations of clouds, for the heavens are least interesting when they are pure and perfect. Clouds are what makes the sunrise and sunset brilliant and dramatic.

Can the same be said of other natural phenomena? Doesn't every flower possess a loveliness peculiar to itself, the more so the more closely we examine it? The shapes of trees and their details of leaf, branch, and bark; the changing sounds of a brook as it rushes over rocks on its downward course; the calls and songs of birds—each of these has its peculiar appeal. Certainly every beauty has unique qualities, a distinctive character, and a recognizable degree of value. An orchid may appear more attractive than a violet, the call of a cuckoo more winsome than a crow's. The scale of beauty is a qualitative one, ranging from the pleasant to the profound.

Yet cases appear that are more difficult to assimilate to this benign aesthetic of nature, and for different reasons. The slug leaving behind its trail of slime may fascinate the naturalist but repels most others. The colors of the setting sun may be more varied and striking through the miasma that hovers over a city, but they are a distressing sign of the pollution that produces them. Other states of nature may have even less to redeem them: a perfect Caribbean beach deformed by sand mining into a lunar landscape, or a hill-side stripped of its trees, washing away as we look on. Although one can find aesthetic interest in the texture, color, and light of such landscapes, it is hard to overlook the violence revealed in their barrenness.

One may remark, however, that most of these are unnatural cases, cases in which the human hand has created the problem, that beauty is everywhere in untouched nature, and only when people intervene in the natural process do problems arise. Yet the issue is more complicated than this picture allows: the human presence is unavoidable, not only in the natural world but on the very occasion of beauty. There is little or nothing on this planet that has not been influenced by human action. Not only have people radically altered the earth's surface, but human practices have affected the atmosphere, the seas, the very climate. Moreover, the awareness of beauty and the aesthetic satisfaction this affords are grounded in perceptual experience, a human occurrence. Our recognition and participation are essential in recognizing beauty's presence and indeed for its very possibility.

Nature untouched, then, is a state found exclusively in prehuman history and about which we can only conjecture. It exists now merely as a speculative idea, for a person's awareness is the filter through which both nature's meanings and its beauties are necessarily apprehended. The title of this chapter is therefore not a conflict of opposites but somewhat ironic, since nature, as we know it, and human action, as we have just seen, are not different realms but the same. They are cited as the subject of my discussion and not as an implied contrast.[2]

The observation is well made that our appreciation of nature has developed historically. What was once regarded as fearsome wilderness, forests of lurking danger that should be avoided, has come to be seen as a place to admire and enjoy. The historicity of nature applies not only to our appreciation and to the meanings we discern but to the forms of nature as well. The landscapes we inhabit are cultural landscapes, their shapes, vegetation, and processes influenced by the characteristic living patterns of the people who dwell in them. These patterns themselves vary historically and change with new technologies. We can see this not only in urban scenes but also in agricultural landscapes and in the countryside as a whole. Furthermore, as we now realize too well, human intervention has redistributed many species and exterminated many others. Nature alone is therefore a fiction; even in its wildest places, nature is always culture.

Yet the spectrum of nature includes more than open and cultivated landscapes. We must come to terms with nature remade: the natural scene transfigured by human action into towns and cities, reshaped by dams and irrigation projects, deforested into eroded and barren hills, cleared for farming and then abandoned to reforest itself, abused into deserts and irrigated into lush fields. These too are nature's human landscapes, and in the processes of inhabitation the planet itself has been transformed. New kinds of beauty have appeared, but so has its denial. The landscape humanized by fields and clusters of farm buildings, villages settled at the confluence of rivers or nestled among hills, cities constructed as monuments to the possibilities of a harbor—these may represent forms of mutual fulfillment that create new kinds of environmental value. But if, as Ruskin implies, untouched nature is always beautiful, the nature people have made is not. It ranges across the positive degrees of a continuum of values to cross its neutral point and enter the negative. As there is bad art, bad in different ways, so there is unlovely nature, unlovely in ways that are perhaps unimaginable but unflinchingly real: an automobile graveyard spreading junked cars across the wide folds of a rural hillside; a development of nearly identical houses on a site leveled for convenience into anonymity; a stream crossing an urban region straitened into a concrete channel, buried beneath the pavement, or turned into an open sewer for industrial waste; wetlands filled in to provide room for industry or housing; a lake in a quiet, wooded setting turned into a playground for power boats and water-skiers. Does entertainment value exceed aesthetic value, casual pleasure take precedence over national landscapes, economic interest override the irrecoverable resources embedded in primal wilderness? These considerations raise many issues—political, economic, social, and moral, as well as aesthetic. Human life is a complicated affair, and our actions in the natural world introduce deeply interrelated dimensions of difficulty.

AESTHETIC VALUES IN ART AND NATURE

Aesthetic values take many forms, then, both positive and negative, and they are intermixed with values of other kinds. The issues are complex and conflicts often occur, not only about the variety of values but also about the forms they take and the degree to which they are present. One may wonder, in particular, what the aesthetics of nature has to do with the domain with which aesthetic value is usually associated: the arts. Yet many of the questions about negative value in aesthetics can be asked of artistic as well as human and environmental forms of negativity. One of the features of aesthetic experience, commonly underrated, is its catholicity. The aesthetic ranges over a continuum from positive to negative and is present to some degree in all places and on all occasions. Dewey's critics rarely grasp his recognition of the pervasiveness of the aesthetic character of experience, for the academic tradition has confined it to carefully selected objects on chosen occasions and in special places. Of course, to argue for the omnipresence of the aesthetic is hardly to claim that it is exclusive or always dominant. Clearly it is neither, but the case can be made that all aesthetic occurrences exhibit a basic similarity, whether they involve nature, art, or human relations. Reflecting on the negative in nature and in art, then, can be mutually illuminating, and I will take advantage of this commonality by moving readily between them. This is especially appropriate, since, as we have seen, nature is a human artifact, at times a human art. In discussing art and nature, we are really talking about the same thing.

Negative values arise in the fine arts, as they do in nature. We discover them, for example, when art panders to sentimentality or fails in the requisite skills of material, technique, or style. Like all art, works of negative value involve forms people have fashioned primarily for perceptual appreciation and experienced meanings. Yet such art is not merely less good; it denies itself, contradicting art's very function of leading us into living, illuminating experi-

ence. Kitsch exemplifies this kind of negativity, proffering sentimentality and surface significance as serious art. Art may acquire
negativity, too, when it is inseparable from the uses to which it is
put and when its aesthetic strength is overwhelmed by its social
role, as in the service of repression, persecution, or war.

But it may be that a negative aesthetic is most clearly intelligible
in environment. Even in largely unchanged environments, aesthetic
appreciation occurs in varying degrees. Such values arise when people engage with the landscape. "Full many a flower is born to blush
unseen, and waste its sweetness on the desert air," Gray sang, but
these are only botanical events, except insofar as we see them and
taste their sweetness, or entertain them, as here, in poetic imagination.[3] Moreover, the manner of our entering into the landscape
recognizes differences in aesthetic value. When we choose a scenic
route over a shorter and faster one, select a vacation site, or compose a scene with a camera, we are shaping our experience of nature on aesthetic grounds that recognize degrees of beauty. As with
the arts, the aesthetic value of natural environments varies with the
features of the object and the contribution of the perceiver.

More striking, however, are those cases of environmental experience that have little or nothing to redeem them. These are, unfortunately, not difficult to find, from land surfaces gutted by strip mining
to continuous blocks of plain, uniform high-rise apartment buildings.
We make judgments of aesthetic disvalue just as we do of positive
value, and we recognize differences of degree, but no clear, graduated
scale defines quantitative increments of aesthetic negativity. Moreover, two or more orders of negation may be at work in many
instances—one of morality and another of aesthetics—and within
each mode of disvalue we recognize quantitative and qualitative differences. As in art that may be skillfully and beautifully made but that
has a sadistic subject matter or induces a destructive reaction, positive and negative scales may be implicated simultaneously. In Maine,
lovely low-spreading blueberry fields are treated with the pesticide
Velpar, whose effects are not fully known. Manhattan's Central Park,
an Olmsted and Vaux masterwork, is a magnet to visitors, yet its
secluded areas host violent attacks. Here the aesthetic and the moral
are not only combined but interdependent. Is it the moral factor that

renders the case negative and not just less beautiful? Do instances of negative aesthetics in environment always occur in a moral context, or can the negative be aesthetically (im)pure? Finally, is the negative case in environment different from that in art?

These are not questions easily disposed of, nor does this catalog of negative instances in nature and art provide a foundation for criticism. So let me approach the subject more systematically by considering some modes of negativity as they occur both in the arts and in environment. The modes that follow do not exhaust the possibilities, their order is not a strictly logical one, and my analysis of them is not exhaustive. Still, they represent a range that is broad enough to exhibit the variety and curious complexity of the aesthetically negative.

MODES OF NEGATIVITY

The most obvious case of aesthetic negativity seems to be *the ugly*. To the popular mind, ugliness is the antithesis of beauty. Whereas the one represents what is precious in art and in the appreciation of nature, the other represents its opposite, that which offends precisely by being unattractive. Beauty and ugliness, however, do not provide the proper frame for this discussion. They are not opposites, nor is the ugly necessarily a form of aesthetic negation.

Beauty has several meanings, ranging from a general recognition of aesthetic value to perfection of form. It is with the latter that the ugly stands in contrast, as when Aquinas writes that integrity or perfection (*integritas sive perfectio*) is one requirement for beauty, since what is defective is deemed ugly.[4] Perfection, however, is conceptual, not empirical. It is linked with the classical notion of ideal form, as in Plato's theory of ideas, where the *eidos* is the flawless model that actual things only approximate, and in Aristotle's entelechy, where the achieved form of an organic body that some vitalists have interpreted as a force regulates and directs the development and functioning of living things according to an inherent pattern. For Aquinas, perfection is linked to an argument for God's existence, since gradations of goodness, truth, and nobility in our experience require an ultimate or perfect point from which they can be measured, and God is that perfection.[5]

Experience and its objects invariably fail, by this criterion, since they are never perfect. Yet this is a defect only when one is governed by a conceptual model, not an empirical one. Perfection is an inappropriate standard for nature, not just because the world never attains it but because such an ideal is both irrelevant and misleading. It turns our eyes away from the endless variation and infinite detail of natural experience. It is, in fact, out of this very succession of uniquenesses that the wonder of natural beauty emerges. Perfection is an external measure, chosen on metaphysical, theological, or epistemological grounds but not on empirical or aesthetic ones. So in this sense, nothing in nature is ugly because imperfect, since nothing can be perfect. The straight line, the circle, and other geometrical abstractions are often useful but are rarely if ever found in faultless form in a natural setting. The fascination of natural objects lies in their uniqueness and endless variety. Never perfect, they are, like Ruskin's clouds, nonetheless always beautiful.

But what can be said about such apparently repugnant creatures as rats and snakes, spiders and slugs? Although they find an unsavory place in some folk cultures, they are an acquired distaste and even have their aficionados. What about commonly repulsive objects such as excrement and putrid flesh? The first gave Plato pause in his search for ideal forms, and the second provided food for Baudelaire's sadistic love lyric *Une Charogne,* "A Carrion." Yet both have found a place in art, possibly even good art, in company with "Piss Christ," Rembrandt's side of beef, and Soutine's strangled chicken. For some observers, the cultural mix of morality, folklore, and psychology that surrounds such things may obstruct any aesthetic interest. Yet other experienced and knowledgeable people may recognize that interest. Just as beauty need not be perfection, its recognition need not be universal. Insofar as these objects provide aesthetic value, they merit the claim of beauty in the broadest sense of the term that is synonymous with such value. In nature as in art, the ugly has its beauty.

Perhaps it is the poverty of our negative vocabulary that has led us to take the ugly to represent aesthetic negativity. Shorn of this unseemly obligation, the ugly, like the grotesque, which is one of its special cases, is really a species of positive value. Art, especially in this century, has found inspiration in the ugly, probing its many forms and facets. We need no longer turn only to the gargoyles on Notre-Dame de Paris to exemplify the grotesque; the ugly has bloomed in many other directions: Picasso's sculptural wrinkles on the head of an old woman, Soutine's contorted visage of the bellhop at Maxim's, and the virulent slashes of yellow and pink that represent de Kooning's women are a few striking examples. The search for transcendent beauty has been abandoned in our time for a fascination with its other sides.

More genuine forms of aesthetic disvalue occur, though they are not conventionally recognized as such. *The offensive* is one: if the ugly is not unbeautiful, surely it may offend us. Offense occurs in transgressing a rule of taste or behavior in nature and in art, just as it does in equivalent ways in morality and law. Such rules have their origin in custom, and although they may not be arbitrary, they are certainly the victims of circumstance. Moreover, rules in law, art, and morality obviously have different social purposes and functions. They must therefore respond to different considerations, and the ways in which we can offend them are different. Furthermore, the demarcations between these domains are entirely customary, and the interrelations of law, morality, and art are constantly being challenged and redefined, further complicating the nature and scope of their rules.

When art offends, it may insult our moral sense or our aesthetic sensibility. Usually it is the moralist who is offended when artists press against the self-satisfying constraints of convention. Mapplethorpe's photographs of interracial homophilia are the most well known recent example, not yet having had time to be assimilated—like Courbet's *The Awakening*, with its lesbian lovers, or *The Origin of the World*, depicting female genitalia—into the canon.[6] Yet there are times where art can offend on exclusively aesthetic grounds, as when it offers pretension masquerading as profundity. This takes its most common form in kitsch, when artists apply their craft and sensibility to pander to a low taste for sentimentality. At its extreme, kitsch merges with banality, a distinguishable aesthetic disvalue of its own.

When we call commercial strip development offensive, is it on moral or aesthetic grounds? There are no unbreachable aesthetic rules that govern the design of a commercial district, but there are standards of taste, standards related, as Hume pointed out long ago, to the cultivation and capacity of the critic. An aesthetic interest lies in perceptual relatedness, in coherence, perhaps in harmony. The incongruous or obtrusive can have a place, certainly, but when it is aesthetically effective it is assimilated into some larger frame or purpose. Aesthetic offense diminishes us humanly by manipulating us perceptually in the interest of other ends, by exploiting our susceptibilities, by engineering measured anxieties to impair our judgment, or by creating sheer discomfort. No absolute reigns here, to be sure, for even a practiced eye may inconceivably find charm in Las Vegas, but a preponderance of expert judgment is all we need in an aesthetic realm that is responsive to custom and change. And is this any less authoritative than the custom that underlies law and morality?

What is aesthetically offensive in strip development is not the self-defeating character of marketing hyperbole, where visual shrillness drowns all perceptual discrimination in an ocean of overstimulation. The aesthetic affront lies in an insensitivity to place or, when the commercial value of place is recognized, in the vulgarization of its attractive features or the imposition of contrived or false ones. A common instance is the exploitation implicit in a fake historical design theme chosen for its emotional and hence its economic value, with little regard for its appropriateness in time and place. Perceptual deception is offensive aesthetically as well as morally. It lulls us with easy pleasantries. It may obscure an aesthetic interest by incoherent visual and architectural features, or it may distract us with exaggerated perceptual qualities while failing to satisfy genuine needs.

Shopping malls provide a different field for offense. They display a complete range of aesthetic value, from malls that simply rectangularize the commercial strip to others that reach toward positive value by an overall design logic and humanize their market function by integrating it with recreational and cultural facilities. Summer cottages whose presence pollutes the scenery of a shoreline are offensive in a different way; the builders place personal indulgence over the commonly acknowledged attractiveness of an uncluttered and natural landscape, despoiling the very qualities that originally made the area attractive.

A related form of aesthetic negativity is found in art and design that offend us because they lack the fresh force of creative imagination and acquiesce in a conventional style, subject matter, or sentiment. Such failure can be called *the banal*. Art that is trite is doubly disappointing, first because it fails aesthetically—that is, it is flat and ineffective in appreciation—and then because it fails as art by not utilizing the capacities of the craft to reveal new possibilities of awareness in perception and imagination. This criterion does not imply that art must always innovate to avoid such a charge, but rather that it must be vital enough, even when repetitive, to attract and even excite fresh attention.

Is nature ever banal? Is the sunset trite because it is overdone, or does it become banal from repetition? Like the conventional artist, nature repeats itself endlessly. Yet our expectations of nature are somewhat different from our expectations of art. Here the wonder lies in the particularity of a common field flower, the texture of a pebble on the beach, the passing glint of light on the water. The interest in the most ordinary occurrences of nature, such as the clouds, lies in their subtle differences and uniqueness or, on another scale, in the qualities of the overall pattern. Although there is a history of styles in appreciating nature, change is not aesthetically necessary. Slow development was once true of the arts, and it might still be if we were not so obsessed by newness and change. A static art is not inevitably banal if it proceeds by refining its technique, subtly varying the style, offering a richness of aesthetic surface and imaginative depth within its chosen range.

The dull may be a consequence of banality, but it is not confined to it. New art can be dull from lack of invention, clumsy technique, or shallow imagination. Such are failures of the artist. Dullness in the appreciation of nature, however, results from the feeble contribution of an unperceptive observer, a lethargic participant. For the excited eye, nothing in nature is ever dull but becomes more fascinating the more closely it is examined. Curiously, when nature is dull, it is through the human touch: plantations of evenly spaced spruce, rows of development houses, a flat lawn with less irregularity than a hand-woven carpet.

A rather different form of disvalue is *the unfulfilled,* which is difficult to judge because it refers not to what is there but to what is not. Its negativity lies as much in our disappointment as in the aesthetic object, since what is present may be of high quality. Unfulfillment is hard to specify, for it is difficult to judge on the basis of what we do not have. Some cases are easy enough, such as unfinished works like the Scherzo of Schubert's B Minor ("Unfinished") Symphony, of which the composer sketched only a few bars. Some works that others have completed, such as Mozart's *Requiem* and Bartók's *Viola Concerto,* are rightly considered masterly, yet one can often detect where the composer's hand faltered and wonder how the music would have sounded had his pen remained steady. Unfulfillment may be an insignificant factor in paintings such as Gilbert Stuart's 1796 portrait of George Washington, which is frequently reproduced with its lower portion still only gessoed,[7] or Turner's seascapes, which the artist was always touching up even when they were on exhibition. Some find in Michelangelo's *Slaves,* struggling to emancipate themselves from their marble blocks, a sculptural power and symbolic significance that are greater perhaps than if the works had been completed. The unfulfilled also applies to good ideas poorly executed, such as an art object inadequately worked out or polished, or art that fails to take advantage of the possibilities inherent in the materials or subject matter, or a richly suggestive idea for a work that is never executed at all.

Can environment be unfulfilled? This is a complex question, considering that people have had a hand, more or less, in every environment. Was the English landscape, which had been deforested over centuries, unfulfilled before Kent, Repton, and Brown shaped it into a pastoral idyll in the early nineteenth century? Could one have known this before the fact? Unfulfillment is often joined with other forms of aesthetic disvalue when one mourns failed opportunities, seeing trailer houses dotting a rural landscape or a ranch house and lawn not far from a native farmhouse on a country road in New England.

What about the effects of war on the landscape? When moral concerns are such a powerful factor in judgment, the aesthetic can easily be overlooked. Yet a strong force in our perceptual disfavor is the loss of agrarian harmony in the landscape and the failure of its productive order. Like an untended garden, the waste in an agricultural landscape left to itself has an aesthetic element.

> Should not in this best garden of the world,
> Our fertile France, put up her lovely visage?
> Alas, she [peace] hath from France too long been chased!
> And all her husbandry doth lie on heaps
> > Corrupting in it own fertility. . . .
> The even mead, that erst brought sweetly forth
> The freckled cowslip, burnet and green clover,
> Wanting the scythe, all uncorrected, rank,
> Conceives by idleness, and nothing teems
> But hateful docks, rough thistles, kecksies, burs,
> Losing both beauty and utility.[8]

There is an aesthetic argument, too, for peace. In industrialized countries, moreover, much of the urban and rural landscape is a condemning witness to scarring misuse and lost possibilities. The aesthetically negative is no simple quantity, and many of the modes I am identifying form complex combinations. Unfulfillment is often a factor when other negative and even positive elements are present.

Closely related to the unfulfilled is *the inappropriate*, where aesthetic failure comes not so much from what is not done as from the unsuitability of a work to its context. A funeral march played for a wedding processional, like a ball gown worn to an afternoon tea, is jarring in context, not in itself. Similarly inappropriate is a house built without regard to the features of its site, or a building that towers irrelevantly above its neighbors or whose design ignores the architectural context and introduces a disruptive disequilibrium. Foreign regional or ethnic designs used without regard to local building traditions never succeed in being at home, such as when a Spanish hacienda or a Swiss chalet is built in a Maine coastal village.

Another form of negativity consists in *trivializing* what is real and important, limiting experience to a petty plane when it could be enlarged into significance. One common form this takes consists in treating matters that are significant and serious as merely casual. Among the arts, film is especially culpable. It often uses current social and personal issues of race, ethnicity, gender, and sex for their popular appeal and glibly exploits their serious content on a superficial plane for purely commercial purposes.

Does environmental design ever trivialize its subject matter? The scope of this question is dangerously broad, for a positive answer could lead to condemning much design and building practice. A themed hotel or restaurant that unimaginatively imitates an earlier architectural style trivializes the past for those who visit or work there by conveying a false sense of history. These cases anticipate a more general sense of the trivial found in treating the genuine needs and values of the human participant in a slick and thoughtless manner. One thinks of the soulless boxlike buildings encouraged by the international style and of the cliché-ridden pastiches that substitute for the playful and imaginative possibilities of postmodernism. Perhaps the one-design development house and the standardized suburb trivialize people's home environment, as these larger buildings do public places. All these diminish the human participant. Shaping an environment that provides enabling conditions for the lives of its inhabitants is a powerful moral responsibility. The tragedy of the trivial rests as much in the failure of opportunity as in what it actually does.

The deceptive carries the negativity of the trivial still farther by introducing an intentional factor. This is what makes artistic forgeries so unpalatable, for although a van Meegeren Vermeer may have some inherent merit, the affront of deceit, not only to the financial interests of the art market but also to the wider art public, brings the opprobrium of the art world down on the offender, along with the punitive arm of the law.[9] The trompe l'oeil painting excites our admiration through its virtuosity rather than our annoyance at having been taken in. Is it the same with architecture? Plastic palaces that imitate solid materials are more than a difference in degree from tromp l'oeil marble mantels and wood-grained moldings. When we discover that a charming white clapboard house or a church in Vermont is covered with aluminum or vinyl siding, we feel foolishly duped and look about for the real thing to satisfy our expectations. Do people notice when their slate countertops are Formica and their dens oak-paneled in plastic? Is there an answer to the defense that no one is deceived for long by these false surfaces and that their low maintenance justifies their use? It is not the materials that are at issue here but the deception. The condemnation lies not in using new building materials but in using them falsely.

Other forms of deception are easier to identify than to judge. What about the false vernacular? Unlike postmodernism, which combines various stylistic features but doesn't disguise the fact or pretend that they are authentic, architecture has long used historical styles freely but less playfully, from nineteenth-century Gothic churches to early-twentieth-century neoclassical museums and government buildings. Most domestic architecture in this country since the middle of the twentieth century ignores indigenous traditions and makes the choice of style as arbitrary as selecting an upholstery fabric—even more so, since in this last instance, the decor of the room is usually taken into account. The New England colonial stands in southern suburbs; the ranch house sits on a suburban street in the East. The most egregious cases of false vernacular occur in theme parks, themed hotels, restaurants, and housing developments, where historical and national styles are chosen with blithe indifference to time, place, and context. At what point does the willing self-deception of the user merge into unthinking acceptance and belief? And what is its influence on children, for whom comparison and judgment are not possible? Deception is particularly troubling in matters of environmental design, for here it is not a matter of a false statement, a book that misrepresents its subject, or a propaganda film. All these are relatively easy to counter by exposure, argument, and disproof. But how does one disprove the false world a person inhabits, especially when there is nothing outside with which to compare it?

Here we move clearly onto moral ground, for the deceptive incorporates a moral issue in the very heart of the aesthetic one. Within this mode of aesthetic negativity, the two are fully interdependent. We regard both the practice and the harmful effects of deception with opprobrium, and nowhere more than in deceptive education. Aesthetic deception undermines people's sense of reality. What is environmental reality when the only thing that is real in people's experience is the false? When history is "Main Street USA" and the American western, science is *Star Wars*, the legal system is *L.A. Law*, and geography and culture are *National Geographic*? At this point the aesthetic shares moral culpability with the other forces of deception.

This sequence of aesthetic negativities leads finally to its most extreme degree: *the destructive.* It may seem odd to apply so strong a word to the aesthetic, which many regard as the wimp of cultural interests. Yet protectors of the social order have long recognized and feared the power of the arts. Censorship is often used in the service of moral convention and political domination, and although it can be self-defeating as a means of control, there are other places where tolerance need not be extended voluntarily simply on principle. Not everyone agrees on what constitutes socially destructive art. Yet such representatives of negativity as ethnic and nationalistic demagogues, priests of moral repression, and purveyors of persecution propose some form of destruction as the means to their end, means in which the aesthetic has a time-honored place. Songs and anthems, posters and dress, theater and ritual, oratory and literature, film and photography are used in the service of every cause, those that undermine as well as those that promote human good. The glorification of these causes in art need not be given a public forum in the name of the free speech that their proponents would revoke. Why should we extend toleration to the intolerant? These comments are not intended to endorse any sort of official board of censors but rather to highlight the fact that the arts have destructive uses and that a negative aesthetics provides the grounds for condemning them. Exposure is a powerful defense.

Environmental design has long been used for repressive ends; that is part of its tradition. From the walls that divided the ancient Chinese commercial city into wards to make crowd control more effective to the harassing design and ostracizing location of public housing today, an antihuman aesthetic has often shaped people's perceptual world and created realities that limit and deny them.[10] Only in recent times has urban design been thought of as a humanizing and liberating force.

AESTHETIC HARM

The destructive appears in many guises. This region of negativity can be given some order by centering further discussion around three interrelated forms: the moral, the social, and the aesthetic.

Moral thought has been preoccupied with regulating and prohibiting actions rather than enabling them. The tradition of Western ethics has been a prescriptive, often negative one, devoted to developing and justifying principles of control, from the Ten Commandments and the Golden Rule to the categorical imperative. One might even regard the very quest for an ethical principle as a search for a rational order of restraint, and the attempt to universalize any such principle as the desire to impose constraint consistently. Even classical utilitarianism, although concerned with promoting people's interests, is regulatory, disregarding peripheral harm in the name of maximizing the quantity of benefit with the abstract impersonality of rational judgment.

Although the socializing role of morality is essential, its humanizing possibilities are largely undeveloped. Yet that tradition is an ancient one. It appears in the ancient Hebrews' responsibility for the indigent and the stranger and in the early Christians' morality of love, and it returns in our own time in the feminist ethic of care. One can understand the need for constraint, yet one wonders about the undeveloped realm of positive ethics, about what forms this might take and how it would answer to criteria different from those of logical order and generalizability. Still, moral belief, both in its theoretical elaboration and in its institutional application, has tended to work as a negative force, controlling, impeding, and imposing on people's actions by precept and edict.

Much has been written recently about socially destructive actions, such as the Holocaust and ethnic cleansing. The social malpractices of the modern world—war, drugs, crime, intolerance, terrorism, repressive power—dominate collective life. These obscure the many small, unsensational acts of cooperation and benevolence that are the true heart of social living. Yet the socially destructive reverses the healthy dynamic equilibrium of a sound society, where the negative is an aberration.

We are, unfortunately, well acquainted with morally and socially destructive actions, and the study of normative negativity must examine them individually and fully. I mention these types of negativity mainly to acknowledge the scope of the destructive, but my concern here is with the aesthetic. Is there such a thing as aesthetic harm? How can something be aesthetically destructive?

Aesthetic harm, at the very least, is the denial of sensory richness and perceptual fullness. It takes a more assertive form in perceptual conditions that desensitize people, that impede, impair, or diminish human capacities for experience. Harm here occurs at the most basic level of the aesthetic, whose roots lie in perceptual experience. But the aesthetic becomes refined as factors are added—the kinds of factors that are most developed in the arts. Among these are fineness of discrimination, the enhancement and enlargement of perception, the awareness of sensory relationships, the vital engagement of intense appreciation, the grasping of embodied meanings, the expansion of what is called, poetically, the human spirit. Aesthetic harm undermines these. It coarsens perceptual consciousness, constricts the development of sensory awareness and the pulsing vitality of the body, and promotes sensory depravity. Aesthetic harm thus demeans the values and meanings embedded in that complex functioning we call human experience. Moreover, the distortion or restriction of perceptual experience manipulates and misleads our sense of reality. Extremes of deprivation or excess and disorienting misdirection can cause madness or death. All these are kinds of aesthetic harm.

Aesthetic harm can be distinguished from such other modes of negativity as the dull and the trivial by the seriousness of its effects.

This may occur in different ways. The harm caused by lack is one way, by the deprivation of the values found in deepened and enlarged perceptual experience. An aesthetically impoverished landscape diminishes its inhabitants, surrounding people with the bland uniformity of slum, urban, or suburban housing, with littered streets and empty lots filled with refuse, with desperate tufts of grass and scraggly bushes, or with the predictable plantings and arbitrarily curved streets of suburban developments. Those who inhabit such places know nothing else but a contracted world and suffer the impoverishment of a spirit denied.

Aesthetic harm also occurs by imposition. It comes in the inescapable noise of traffic, factories, lawn mowers, and canned music; in vehicular exhaust gases, industrial smoke, chemical odors, and the blue wisps of burning tobacco. Even the sense of taste is unavoidably polluted by excessive sugar and salt, exaggerated flavors, and extravagant quantities of cheap sauces. The visual pollution of the landscape is omnipresent and unavoidable in the blight of telephone poles and lines, the bland oppressiveness of most skyscrapers, the random punctuation of transmission towers and TV satellite dishes, and the ravages of mining and clear-cutting on the surface of the land. But the harm of aesthetic presence is probably most overwhelming in the strident signage of commercial strips in urban areas and of billboards in the countryside.

Is there aesthetically offensive behavior? The aesthetic harm found in individual actions is elusive, perhaps because it is more personal and easier to overlook in oneself. Among the things to consider here are loud voices, heavy perfume, tobacco smoke, the various forms of inconsiderate behavior that offend our sensibilities, including our aesthetic ones. Of course, this must be qualified culturally. In some circles, loud laughter and a radio played at high volume outdoors are proper enjoyment; in others, they are crude and insensitive. This poses a problem mainly when such circles overlap, as in a restaurant or in contiguous neighborhoods. But social living creates many such conditions. Which sensibility should take priority? Questions of etiquette raise similar questions, for they involve social aesthetics as much as they do ethics. Moreover, the destructive as a mode of negativity raises a tantalizing question: just as the aesthetic can generate a moral critique, can it also ground a positive morality?[11]

THE NEGATIVE SUBLIME

One further domain of negativity remains to be discussed here. In traditional aesthetics, the sublime denotes an extreme degree of value whose force exceeds the measured proportions of the beautiful. Like beauty, the sublime inhabits the aesthetic because it reflects the direct encounter with a thoroughly perceptual content. Yet its distinction and fascination lie precisely in the experience of incommensurability. The sublime rests on an experience of power and magnitude so overwhelming that it cannot be circumscribed. Kant, whose discussion of the sublime is best known, associated it not with art but with nature manifested in the uncontrollable power of the sea in a storm and the magnitude of the starry sky.

Why have we returned with renewed interest to this notion, developed largely within the traditional aesthetic of the eighteenth century? I suspect that in part, it may be because the sublime is the aesthetic category that captures most compellingly the dominant perception, in sense and in meaning, of our lived world. But that world is not the world of nature, a world whose greatness evoked humility in Kant. We live in a vastly different one in which the power of nature, though still awesome, has been cast into insignificance by the unbounded power that lies, barely controlled, in human hands. Order has slipped into chaos, rationality has been undermined, certainties have degenerated into probabilities, and absolutes have died along with God.

We have not developed new cognitive structures and social institutions to deal with these changes in knowledge and understanding. Instead, societies have succumbed to the influence of demagogues of the Left and the Right, producing the totalitarian state, mass production, mass marketing, mass culture, and mass murder. We face the plague of AIDS, the glacier-like threat of an expanding world population, and the still present threat of nuclear annihilation. The corporate amoeba, scientifically engineered to a size and power that allows it to engulf the human personality and absorb human consciousness, is gradually assimilating the national state and monopolizing the productive process and the economic order of the entire planet. Most people are no longer aware of the starry heavens that so awed Kant that he took them to exemplify the sublime. The glow of light from our cities renders the stars quite invisible.

No longer is it nature, then, that exemplifies the sublime, as it did when viewed from mountaintops and stormy coasts in the eighteenth century; it is the human environment. This is not just an environment of towering edifices but a cultural environment of towering institutions whose power is so great that it cannot be conceived directly and concretely and exceeds our capacity to grasp it rationally. Such an environment exemplifies the sublime precisely because it cannot be grasped, because it is unpresentable. It is the sublime of excess, not of the positive but of the negative. The negative sublime has, in fact, become the dominant aesthetic consciousness of our age.[12]

THE SCOPE OF NEGATIVITY

This discussion has ranged widely, though no more so than the negative aesthetic itself, and matters have become somewhat clearer. One of them is that the modes of negativity, from the banal to the destructive, are found equally in environment and in the arts. Instances of one illuminate and support the case for the negative in the other. Certainly there are differences, but they are more of individual cases than of genres. Rather than setting art and environment in opposition, it is more useful to examine particular forms and occurrences of aesthetic negativity wherever they occur.[13] Moreover, the modes of negative aesthetics are many, and these reflections have left some of them untouched. Whether the grotesque and the boring, for example, can be understood as variants of the ugly and the dull or as separate categories needs further thought. And how should one deal with the bland, the insipid, and the vulgar? Obviously, we can analyze the individual modes of aesthetic negativity differently and debate particular instances. Rather than vitiating the case for the negative, this ability acknowledges it.

What is important is to make such negativity explicit. This means realizing that aesthetic value has a negative range and that it occurs in identifiable modes that we can apply to environment and the arts in ways that lead to specific judgments. What complicates the task is that the modes are not all on the same footing. Each occupies a different place in an order of negativity, yet that order is not immediately apparent. It clearly cannot assume a linear, one-dimensional progression. Indeed, the order of negativity is not mathematical at all but rather takes the form of a normative complex, another matter that needs examination. Furthermore, the scope of aesthetic negativity itself is unclear. Even the positive end of the spectrum is not inviolate. Can there be too much good taste? Can things be too perfect? Is aesthetic excess itself a kind of negativity? One may yearn for irregularity, for rough edges, for the unpredictable, like the surface depression deliberately pressed into the otherwise perfect roundness of a Japanese teapot or the subtle differences in the repetitive pattern of a Persian rug.

AESTHETIC AND MORAL VALUES

Perhaps the most troublesome and complex issue of all concerns the interrelation of the aesthetic and the moral, a question raised early in this chapter and one that a discussion of negativity cannot avoid. We face this issue directly when we attempt to judge the aesthetic component in art that is considered degraded or degenerate. The aesthetic and the moral are equally central here. Despite a feeling of moral repugnance, we recognize the aesthetic and want to be able to acknowledge its own value. Yet at the same time we are troubled by the fact that this aesthetic value may be inseparable from the moral message. Can something that is morally negative ever be aesthetically pure? Conversely, do instances of negative aesthetics invariably possess a moral dimension? Is moral condemnation the basis of aesthetic negativity, or is it distinguishable and separate?

Each mode and instance of the negative requires its own answer. In some of its forms, the disvalue may be primarily aesthetic, even though a moral element is present. This is the case with the failure of aesthetic opportunities in the banal, the dull, the unfulfilled, and the inappropriate, which, by disappointing human good, become a moral as well as an aesthetic loss. In other modes, such as the trivializing and the deceptive, a moral presence may dominate the aesthetic and diminish its effect. In the destructive and the negative sublime, the moral component is even more serious, but it still may not overwhelm the aesthetic one. In other modes not developed here, such as the degrading and the degenerate, the moral content may overpower any aesthetic consideration altogether. Yet even here the aesthetic is not entirely displaced, and this raises the issue of their conflict most pointedly.

What emerges from reviewing the range of aesthetic negativity is that a moral content is present to some degree in each of its modes. Even when an aesthetic interest is most pronounced, the moral is never altogether absent. Conversely, although not with perfect symmetry, an aesthetic element may occupy a vestigial place in a moral situation, even though its author may claim more for it. Is the importance of the aesthetic in *The Tropic of Cancer* different from that in *The Story of O*? Determining the degree of imbalance is a task for responsible criticism. Although we should discriminate carefully in exposing the interrelationship of the moral and the aesthetic in the different modes of negativity and their interplay in particular cases, the variety and complexity of instances make it unlikely that we can develop any general rules. The character and degree of negativity depend on the individual mode and the specific instance. The art in judging art becomes even more delicate at the intersection of the moral and the aesthetic.

The presence of a moral dimension reinforces the claim for the significance of aesthetic value. It also makes unacceptable the view that such value can be dismissed as inconsequential or undiscussable on the grounds that it is purely personal. Quite the contrary. The aesthetic offers a basis for social criticism precisely because it, like morality, is grounded in experience that is similar in basic ways. This is complicated by the fact that, again like the moral, aesthetic experience always takes place in a cultural realm having a history and a tradition, and where its value is ultimately judged collectively. The omnipresence of a moral component confirms and reinforces the social character of such experience.

All this is explicit in the negative aesthetics of environment, for environment is visibly common and shared. Values inhere in the human environment, whether it has been consciously designed or not, and aesthetic value, along with moral, political, and economic ones, is an inseparable component. By exposing its presence and developing its interrelationships with these other values, an aesthetic critique can have great force and provide the grounds for a distinctive commentary on environmental proposals and actions. An expanded sense of the aesthetic and a vocabulary of its negative modalities are therefore essential.

POSITIVE ENVIRONMENTAL VALUES

A discussion of negativity runs the risk of identifying the negative with those things associated with it. But it would be a mistake to infer that the human touch always causes nature to wilt. There is an affirmative side to this complex scale of aesthetic value, and it is good to acknowledge it, for we can discover models of how natural processes fulfill some of their inherent possibilities and gain aesthetic richness through a guiding hand. England and France, for example, have characteristically looked on nature as a garden needing to be cultivated. Sharply different garden traditions have led to different cultural landscapes, yet at their best they reflect in contrasting ways a harmonious fusion of natural and human forces. Lancelot Brown's reshaping of the English landscape is one way of cultivating nature, just as Japanese and Chinese gardens integrate the human and the natural through distinctly different sensibilities. Even within national traditions one finds successful variety. The geometrical order of Le Nôtre's gardens at Versailles hardly resembles the informal groves, ponds, and plantings in the Jardins Albert-Kahn in Paris. A less deliberate blending of human actions and natural processes occurs in unexpected places: a road that hugs the contours of the land instead of forcing its way across it; a farmhouse and buildings that complete their site; a port town that embraces its harbor. In such cases, the designers—known or unknown, working individually or collectively—are environmental artists who respected and responded to the demands of their materials with imagination, sensitivity, and affection.

It is a mistake, then, to regard human environmental acts as invariably negative aesthetically, for there are numerous forms and instances of successful collaboration with natural conditions. When negativity does occur, however, we can usually locate its source in careless, unconsidered, narrow, selfish, or deliberately exploitative actions. It would be tempting to say that the natural world, left alone, would always be beautiful. But that is too simple and sentimental a view, for without a human presence, there would be no appreciation of beauty and no awareness of value. So we must be content with the far more difficult matter of directing our necessary environmental presence toward activities that are aesthetically positive. William Morris's well-known comment recognizes the primary importance of the larger sphere: unless people care about carrying on their business without making the world hideous, how can they care about art?

I have not considered directly all the questions raised at the outset, yet some interesting things have emerged. It has become clear that a human presence is necessary for aesthetic awareness to occur and aesthetic value to arise. And just as an aesthetic factor can be discerned in all experience of environment, this is even more clearly true of moral value, which comes, like the aesthetic, from the very presence of people in their social context. With both moral and aesthetic value always implicated, the question of whether they can be dealt with separately is misguided. Types of value have no ontological locus beyond human experience, and discerning their differences is always empirically grounded and historically relative. Enlarging the aesthetic to accept subject matter and experience that are openly sensual, for example, has lessened the influence of conventional morality and has led to intense dispute over their overlapping claims. A newer debate has developed over the acceptability of violence on television, in film, and in performance art. And a growing awareness of ethnicity and the categorial revisions of feminist scholarship have redefined and extended the meaning and scope we give to the moral and the aesthetic in still different ways.

It was a false aesthetic, then—false in its exclusiveness and limits—for the picturesque traveler in the late eighteenth century to find unalloyed aesthetic delight in the decaying cottages and ragged inhabitants of the countryside. And it is just as false for us to ask whether *Triumph of the Will* is a beautiful film independent of its Nazi ideology and propagandistic purposes. It is not the moral factor that renders these cases negative while leaving their beauty untouched. Moral repugnance affects their aesthetic value as well. To isolate these modes of value is an intellectual indulgence unconnected with human experience.

Although this chapter has explored the negative, my intent in writing it was not a Baudelairean perverseness that delights in undermining the sanctity of the aesthetic. Nor did the choice of subject stem from a logical compulsion to conceptual symmetry that must balance the positive value generally associated with the aesthetic by its obverse. My purpose was a constructive one. As the range of aesthetic value has enlarged in recent theory beyond the beauty of art and nature to include the many other forms that human activity takes, aesthetic criticism has the potential to become a powerful intellectual tool for understanding the world we have created. We are all too conscious of the negative at a time when growing material abundance has been overwhelmed by a still more rapid increase in the degree and kinds of threat. To grasp more fully what these dangers are and how better to proceed, we need strong instruments for analysis and judgment. An enlarged aesthetic is one of them.

CHAPTER FIVE

Aesthetic Function

Ever since the eighteenth century, when aesthetics finally discovered that it had an identity of its own, the hallmark of that identity has been disinterestedness. Centering on sense perception, aesthetic theory somehow had to provide an intellectual justification for the emerging independence of the arts by ensuring that they would no longer be subservient to religious, moral, political, or cognitive purposes. Art now was significant not only for its contribution to the princely purposes of church or state; it had to pursue its own course, fulfill its own ends, and offer its own contribution to the life of a culture unhampered by outside obligations. At this moment in history it seemed clear that both identity and protection for the newly designated fine arts could be found in the notion of aesthetic disinterestedness. The consequence of this has been that most Western philosophers of art, from the eighteenth century to the present day, have taken disinterestedness and the host of related notions it has spawned—isolation, contemplation, autonomy, intransitivity, dehumanization, and psychical distance—as aesthetic axioms or, more accurately perhaps, aesthetic dogmas.[1] In one way or another, our encounter with art had to be kept from being confused with the world of practical affairs. To use Kant's influential formulation, we must exclude interest, with its concomitant desire for the pleasant and the good, from aesthetic value, for "taste in the beautiful is alone a disinterested and free satisfaction; . . . no interest, either of sense or of reason, here forces our assent."[2]

Yet the notion of disinterestedness has not enabled art to achieve the autonomy for which it has been searching. As a concept, disinterestedness is actually derivative, since it embodies the classical model of the cognitive attitude as a contemplative ideal.[3]

Furthermore, it shares this dependency with nearly every other theoretical concept in aesthetics. In fact, conceptual dependence and metaphor have been so prevalent in aesthetic theory that it is useful to describe such proposals as surrogate theories, theories that misrepresent art and our experience of it with substitute concepts and half-truths. Such is the case with notions of meaning, symbol, and feeling and with theories of art as communication, imitation, form, and expression.[4]

Moreover, this freedom that aesthetics attempted to procure was a dubious freedom. Emancipation meant isolation, and until well into the twentieth century, the arts pursued for the most part their own course, unmindful of the role they played in the social dynamic. Yet artists act in ways that are oblivious of philosophical decrees, and in each successive age the various arts, despite the proclamations of independence, have explored new regions of sensibility and achieved new types and levels of human and social awareness. It has become increasingly clear that disinterestedness is an overextended idea and that the autonomy of art and the independence of aesthetic theory cannot be gained at the cost of isolation and general irrelevance.

The modern arts have tended to reaffirm the connections and involvement of art, and an idea that helps characterize this is the idea of function. Function here, however, is not a simple maxim, nor is it synonymous with utility. Rather, it describes the place that art occupies in the larger context of social activity. Function is not simply a replacement for disinterestedness: it signifies the radical shift from an aesthetics of contemplation, which characterizes the appreciative observer by a psychological attitude, to an aesthetics of engagement, which points to an active, somatic, multisensory involvement in the aesthetic field. By examining the idea of function more closely, we can see how this has come about.

MECHANICAL FUNCTION

Perhaps the narrowest, most literal case of function is that of an object adapted to a specific task that it performs with a maximum economy of movement and a minimum of wasted effort. The paradigm of this is the machine, and function can be described in this limited sense as *mechanical function*. At the same time as it epitomizes function, the machine, by virtue of the demand for efficiency that is placed on it, might appear at first to be the ultimately unaesthetic object. By meeting its obligations for activity that produces results with maximum economy, the machine exemplifies use and practice. No thought is given to imagination, delight, or any other quality for its own sake, but every attention is devoted to its external end of productive results.

Yet by a strange irony, this very fact of the machine's extrinsic value has contrived to generate intrinsic qualities that are aesthetic. Instead of being quarantined for its dirty hands and mundane thoughts, the machine has succeeded in penetrating the sanctity of our temples of art to demand aesthetic attention. We find that it is impossible to turn back the clock and confine ourselves to the products of the artist's craft. The machine, particularly the industrial machine, has pierced the very heart of human activities to affect the arts themselves.

The machine has come to play a multifaceted role in art. It appears as the subject matter of art in Léger's industrialized human forms, Honegger's aural locomotive *Pacific 231,* and the work of such groups as the Italian Futurists and the Russian Constructivists. Here the image of the machine, the movement of the machine, the transforming power of the machine, and perhaps, as with some of the dadaists, the criticism of the machine form the basis of the perceptual object. Influencing art from a different direction, the machine serves as a supplier of parts and materials and, at times, collaborates with the artist in producing the work. It provides the architect with steel girders and prestressed concrete modules, the composer with tape recorders and synthesizers, the sculptor with sheet metal and acetylene torches, and the playwright with moving stages and elaborate lighting and set-changing machinery. Then there is mechanized art itself, in which the machine serves as a dynamic model for the artist to emulate, as in the cubist's geometrization of nature, or which co-opts the machine for its own purposes, as in kinetic sculpture.

These uses of the machine as artistic subject matter, as a source of materials, as a creative force, and as an artistic model lead with little effort to the machine product and the machine itself as an art object. This is the case not only with the influence of the Bauhaus on design and graphics but also with stylistic movements such as optical art and minimal art and music, which derive their aesthetic dimensions from simplicity, regularity, and repetitive patterns of machine products. It is the case, too, with artists such as Francis Picabia and Max Ernst, many of whose drawings and paintings look like engineer's blueprints, with Duchamp's ready-mades, Tinguely's playful machines, Bugatti's automobiles, and the wide range of mechanical devices that populate the plastic arts.

What, then, are the qualities that the machine and its products embody? They offer accuracy, exactness, and precision of operation. They provide dependability of performance and a uniform, standardized product. Their effort to achieve ever greater efficiency of operation leads to a simplicity and regularity of design, the use of repeated patterns, and reproducibility of both the machine and its product. Finally, there is a striving for the perfect adaptation of the mechanical object to its assigned task in the name of economy of operation. The notion of function encompasses all these features.

Mechanical function thus possesses a double appeal: it is eminently practical, yet eminently pleasing in its own right. Regarded from the standpoint of production, mechanical function is perfect utility; regarded from the standpoint of perception, it is an aesthetic ideal. An aesthetic of function emerges, then, out of the very principle of the machine. It is an ideal embodied in the synthesis of production and perception, like the functional operation of the sailing vessel and the airplane, the smooth workings of the watch and the engine, good form in the racehorse, and perfect timing in the trapeze act. The aesthetic of mechanical function finds its widest fulfillment in design, in architecture, and in city planning.[5]

ORGANIC FUNCTION

A rather different sense of function is based on a biological model. *Organic function* involves more than a collocation of parts designed to work together to fulfill an external task. It is characterized by an integrity in which all the component elements maintain a harmonious equilibrium by adapting reciprocally to one another. Organic function goes beyond mere interrelatedness; it requires cohesion and mutual responsiveness, which make the function of the whole something over and above the action of the parts. This sense of function cannot be described analytically by its elements alone but only through reciprocal relationships. Moreover, unlike mechanical function, where the ends are imposed externally, organic function generates its own ends: an internal dynamic force impels the organism along its own course to fulfillment.

As the machine epitomizes mechanical function, so the human body epitomizes organic function. At this stage of biological science, little has to be said about the functional unity of the organism. The puzzles that still remain have more to do with the few exceptions to the functional standard than with its instances, and these probably have an evolutionary explanation. When the human body is taken as the subject matter of art, its functional qualities usually demand to be acknowledged. Often they determine both the direction in which an art develops and the quality of particular styles. The history of painting in the Renaissance illustrates how different aspects of the body impose requirements of their own on the painter. The discovery of its mass by Giotto, its muscularity by Michelangelo, its linear extension by El Greco, its vital sensuousness by Titian all reveal qualities of the body that find their fullest realization through the "insatiable appetite for the nude" in the sixteenth century. Indeed, the nude as a subject of art, or as a form of art, as Kenneth Clark has called it, can never abandon the functional necessities of the human organism in searching for the ideal. Shape, proportion, and the disposition of the figure all demand to be taken account of.[6]

It is in dance, however, that the organic functionalism of the body is developed most fully. Here the human organism and its movements are not only the primary subject of dance but also the material from which the art is fashioned. Just as formal imbalance in a sculpture produces a sensation of physical imbalance in the onlooker, so in dance the audience tends to participate somatically. We join with the dancer in a common activity, moving in empathetic harmony through the same space and using gestures that have common significance. Choreographers and critics alike agree that the appreciative experience of dance requires a sympathetic kinesthetic response.[7] The body functions as an organism at its fullest and freest in dance, yet it is a functioning that explores not just the body's physical capacities through twisting, turning, stretching, and leaping but also its biosocial range through lifting, carrying, embracing, and moving in tandem in a shimmering iridescence of interrelationships. As the successful nude in painting must evoke at least a trace of erotic feeling, so in the dance pure form and line are impossible.[8] The human body has so powerful an attraction and reaches us on so fundamental a level that the art that uses it can invoke its full reach of mood, emotion, motive, and function.[9] We perceive the body aesthetically precisely through its ability and ease in performing its functions.

In paralleling the organic functionalism of the body as the subject and material of art, the dance appreciator contributes her or his own organic unity of function. Our involvement is multisensory, with all the bodily senses participating in a harmonious synthesis. This synesthetic participation includes the tactile sense, which aesthetics has traditionally excluded because its relation to objects is too close and practical.[10] The functional unity of appreciative perception in dance is not just biological and sensory but also involves psychological and cognitive factors. Their indivisibility has a parallel in the unity of subject and form in the art object and their dynamic integration in perception. All this suggests a still more inclusive unity of perceiver and object in a phenomenal field.[11]

PRACTICAL FUNCTION

The most common way in which people relate to things is in practical situations, and it is precisely here that art has traditionally parted company with objects that are not exclusively aesthetic. *Practical function* involves a context of use in which an object joins with a person in a relation of means to ends. Things here do not delight in themselves; their attraction lies wholly in the uses to which they can be put. This is the interested attitude in its most unalloyed form, which aesthetics has always taken pains to exclude, for it seems to deny in a clear and unequivocal way the intrinsic qualities of aesthetic experience.

It is interesting to notice, however, how difficult it has always been to keep aesthetic involvement unsullied by practical interest. Before the eighteenth century, it was common to see the arts as part of cultural celebrations. Music, dance, painting, and literature were important contributors to religious worship, state ceremonies, and the other ritualistic observances that mark the significant occasions in every society. Even after it proclaimed its autonomy, art continued its social contribution, often in the form of critical commentary, from the comedies of manners of Congreve and Wilde to the satirical paintings and sculptures of Goya and Daumier.

Nevertheless, it is precisely this separation of the fine from the practical arts that must be questioned. Is practical function as sharply removed from the aesthetic as it is generally thought to be? If disinterestedness can be challenged as the proper aesthetic attitude, perhaps its correlate, interest, must also be reexamined. And then we must also question the antithesis of fine and practical art. Beauty, as Emerson once pointed out, must come back to the useful arts. The distinction between the fine and the useful arts must be forgotten. In fact, in the domain of function, he claimed, the beautiful rests on the foundations of the necessary. Nor was Emerson the first to note this. Hume had already observed that utility in certain practical objects becomes the source of their beauty.[12]

It is worth remarking here that the distinction between the fine and the practical arts is a philosopher's distinction, not the artist's. The activity of artistic creation is itself a synthesis of the aesthetic and the practical, where skill at fashioning art objects fuses with perceptual involvement in a mutually responsive way, and both processes are often apparent in the finished work. Furthermore, artists observe no such boundaries in their work, freely crossing and recrossing the lines between literature and journalism, painting and illustration, sculpture and design. There are many instances in which practical and aesthetic interests are so combined as to be inseparable, as in clothing, interior decoration, and simple tools and utensils. Ordinary, cheap hand pliers, for example, achieves its formal aesthetic qualities from the ease with which one can grip and use it as much as from its visual symmetry.

However, the most outstanding instance of the creative amalgam of the practical and aesthetic lies in architecture, where function is coextensive with the achievement of beauty. Mies van der Rohe observed that wherever technology reaches its real fulfillment, it transcends itself into architecture. Pier Luigi Nervi believed that the correct structural solution is the basis of good design and is the best aesthetic solution. Louis Sullivan's famous maxim that form follows function became the starting point for virtually all of modern architecture, although its inherent ambiguity makes it a difficult guide to follow. In the hands of less talented advocates, it has often degenerated into a trite formula, and in those of its opponents, into a straw man.

What is particularly pertinent here about architecture as the exemplar of practical function is that it joins together the art object—the building—with the perceiver—its user—in the interest of complete utility. This is not simply a narrow, utilitarian unity of perceiver and object, however, for when a building works well, in the fullest sense of the term, it achieves aesthetic as well as practical success. Working well is more than a matter of providing useful spaces and convenient avenues for movement in which to carry on the activities that the building was designed to accommodate. It includes those less tangible qualities that transform a structure offering protection from the weather and security for equipment into a congenial human environment: the quality of light, the control of sound, the colors and textures of its surfaces. Functional success treats space as providing the room necessary not just for physical activity but also for the spirit to expand, through such features as open vestibules, lofty ceilings, and broad corridors. When an office building, a school, or a house becomes a humanized environment for carrying on with ease the practical activities for which it was designed, a beauty of operation develops that is at the same time a beauty of living. Architecture is not just an art of interior spaces; it is an art of exterior masses as well, and here, too, function plays an integral part. A building must work well in relation with its site and surroundings; consequently, architecture joins with landscape architecture and city planning in the interest of achieving a fuller and more coherent sense of function. Furthermore, like other conceptual separations in aesthetics, the division in architecture between interior and exterior is disappearing, as new materials and techniques provide greater strength with less bulk, and masonry walls fall before steel and glass. As architecture's practical function improves, its artistic success often increases. Carried further still, the architectural environment illustrates how the mechanical function of a building and the organic function of the human body can be absorbed and synthesized to achieve an end that is as aesthetic as it is utilitarian.

By pursuing the place of function in the arts, we have come to recognize traits of aesthetic experience that have often been overlooked or denied. Central to these is the notion of art as a kind of activity that engages both the art object and its perceiver, bringing them together in a mutually fulfilling transactional relationship. Although the machine, dance, and architecture may not seem to represent the perceptual modes of the other arts, they do challenge traditional models of disinterestedness, isolation, and permanence. They stand, in fact, as better illustrations of what the experience of art does involve. Art is not merely an activity; it is an activity that embraces qualities of our world that traditional aesthetics has often ignored: its mechanical and industrial features, its biological and sensuous elements, and most of all, the intimate participation of the arts in the distinctively human cultural environment. It is difficult to isolate the art object and view it disinterestedly when its force comes from the many ways in which art functions in human culture. There is a kind of contradiction between isolation and import.

The sequence of artistic and aesthetic functions I have explored is not merely a series of alternative meanings. A relationship holds among these different modes. There is an order of subsumption in which each kind of function includes and develops what has come before. Thus organic function adds elements of vital harmony and self-generation to the austere efficiency of mechanical function, and practical function embraces both in a fuller context of interrelation and dependence, where art object and aesthetic subject, engaging in a creative exchange, are functionally inseparable. Most significant, perhaps, is that in moving beyond the description of aesthetic appreciation as an attitude to an analysis of it as a functional activity, we come finally to a kind of function that is most inclusive and offers the most fulfilled account—humanistic function.

HUMANISTIC FUNCTION

This last sense of the notion of function, *humanistic function*, includes the practical but goes well beyond it. Here the interest in the object as a means to an external end is replaced by the object as a *medium* in relation to which we, as participants, can function with the fullest range, intensity, and purity of experience.[13] Yet humanistic function denotes not just a relation but the entire setting, the aesthetic field, within which there is an experiential merging of the perceiver and the object of art in a creative perceptual exchange. Here function becomes active participation, combining the mechanical, organic, and practical aspects of the art object and the aesthetic perceiver into a living movement of intrinsic, primary experience. From this, a synthesis of aesthetic perception, social relevance, and human fulfillment develops into a cultural environment in which each of these not only encompasses the others but also becomes inseparable from them.

As a humanistic process, then, art fuses the artist, the object, and the appreciator in a rich unity of common activity. This function has always existed, though in a dormant state, in the way that action painting gave a central place to Roger Fry's perceptive observation decades earlier that the drawn line is the record of a gesture. Many recent developments in the arts make the humanistic function of art explicit: from the "functional image"[14] of optical art, to relief sculptures, which require the reflected image and movement of the spectator to complete them; from theater, which absorbs the audience into the performance, as in the Living Theatre, the Open Theatre, and the Polish Lab Theatre, to film, which has "re-established that dynamic contact between art product and art consumption," molding the opinions, taste, language, dress, behavior, and physical appearance of an immense public;[15] from the religious experience of the medieval cathedral, which creates a multimedia sensory environment, fusing architecture, sculpture, painting, poetry, drama, and music and extending even to the senses of taste and smell, to the art of community planning, which offers the most inclusive setting for an audience composed entirely of actors in an environment with neither stage nor walls to provide a way of living that will allow men and women to become fully human.[16] Out of these and more, art has emerged as a vital and inclusive activity. The full range of human experience converges then in the aesthetic of a cultural environment to attain its greatest self-realization and most complete consummation. This is aesthetic function at its most complete, the condition of being most human.

❖ CHAPTER SIX ❖

Environment and the Body

HUMAN EMBODIMENT

One might expect that a philosophy of environment would both begin and end with the fact of human embodiment. Such a philosophy can hardly do otherwise. Yet while embodiment frames the discussion, it raises the critical questions; it does not resolve them. What is this body, and what is its relation to other things? What is the meaning and place of consciousness in such an approach? These are troublesome matters.

To start from the body both is a distortion and implies a distortion. It is a distortion because it singles out a particular form from all existence, the human body, and considers it from a human vantage point. This, however, is a contingent condition: the choice of the human form as the exemplar of body is but another instance of the readiness to project human characteristics onto the world at large and construe the world on that model. A second kind of distortion is a necessary one, since we cannot see the world from any standpoint but the human one, projected either as an ideal observer or as an anthropomorphic deity, or concretely as a historically, culturally, and socially situated person.

Speaking of body, moreover, implies a further distortion, in that it suggests that there are things that can be identified that are *not* bodies. Traditionally, these take the form of ideas, mental entities, or constructs that are usually given some separate, independent status. Yet ideas are always embedded in some way, actually in the brain process we uncritically call thinking or consciousness, and potentially in written or other physical form, incomplete as ideas until they are actualized in reflection or discourse. For a philosophy of the body, then, any ideal realm is the disembodied idea of embodied thought.

There are still other difficulties in speaking of the body, difficulties shared by every attempt to distinguish and order things. In trying to specify what we mean by body and how the body relates to the world it inhabits, we find ourselves developing a structure whose divisions demarcate the body from other objects and separate the body from its setting. This is a problem for all discourse and every philosophy, yet it usually goes unobserved, since it seems to be a necessary condition of the conceptual process. But although the philosophical process cannot avoid intruding into the world about which it is reflecting, in a kind of analogue with the principle of indeterminacy, it cannot assume an ontological status for its conclusions. Thus the common divisions of body into diverse and opposed categories—body (abstract) and embodiment (particular), physical object (as the object of science) and material object (as an abstract idea or metaphysical entity), and most prominent, of course, body and mind or spirit—reflect conceptual levels that are often taken to imply ontological ones. In addition, the contrast between human and other forms of embodiment implies a separation that itself conveys a philosophic presumption of difference, discontinuity, and hegemony. Human embodiment has connections to other kinds of body that join with it in a common matrix. But what are the relevant differences among them, where do they lie, and what is the nature of these differences? Can we even speak of body without implying such differences? The main purpose of this chapter is to explore the assumptions involved in these questions.

My body seems most intimately my self. No one—doctor, lover, or beauty specialist—knows it in as much detail and as fully as I do. Yet at the same time, who this body is lies in other people's eyes. From George Herbert Mead to Jacques Lacan, many have argued that we are—we become—the self that we and others see. And what others see, we cannot: not only a reversed, mirror image but also body type, posture, expression, and manner that are directly and unself-consciously present as we ourselves can never know them. Who, then, am I? What am I? Does a Lockean substratum persist, a hidden, "inner" self, once I remove the acquired characteristics of language, behavior, patterns, systems of thought, and even my flesh, whose substance is metabolized out of the kind of food with which my society enables me to sustain my life and nurture my growth?

My body, then, is no pure starting point or simple center. It grows, develops, emerges from, is constructed out of the diverse materials of culture, history, and circumstance. We may say, then, that body is dependent on context, yet body is all we have. This is the beginning and the end of the matter. But what is the nature of that context?

THE BODY AND ITS NATURAL CONTEXT

The native North American peoples often identified their bodies in a literal sense with the land and with the other things, living and not living, whose home is that land.

> Being an Indian means being able to understand and live with this world in a very special way. It means living with the land, with the animals, with the birds and fish, as though they were your sisters and brothers. That is the way we feel about our land. It is our flesh. The grass and the trees are our flesh. The animals are our flesh. This land is our blood. The land gives us life. We still live on the same land as our parents and grandparents, so it is just like they are still living with us. To me the earth is like a mother: She gives life; I am her child. Yes, the earth is a good mother to me, and she is also beautiful. Every day I look at her face and sing in my heart.[1]

This deep connection between body and the land in which they dwell is a common understanding of Native Americans. Their identity with natural place is a literal one: "Every time the white people come to the North or come to our land and start tearing up the land, I feel as if they are cutting up our own flesh, because that's the way we feel about our land. It is our flesh."[2] This association extends beyond the land itself to the natural phenomena that are its processes and to the plants and animals that live in the land.[3] It is part of a view that sees humans as an interrelated part of the natural world and that world as a congruent whole, all parts of which possess value and deserve respect.[4] "The earth and myself are of one mind," affirmed Chief Joseph of the Nez Perce Indians. "The measure of the land and the measure of the earth and myself are of one mind. The measure of the land and the measure of our bodies are the same."[5] Sitting Bull used to say that healthy feet can hear the very heart of Holy Earth.[6]

Such beliefs have been dismissed too often as the animistic imaginings of a primitive mentality. They express, however, a profound understanding of self, not as an internalized consciousness or a deep subjectivity but as an expansive self that recognizes that its identity is bound up with its physical place of inhabitation. Moreover, although articulated with eloquent conviction by Native Americans, such an understanding is not unique to them. From the "dust unto dust" of the Old Testament to the poets and naturalists of recent times, a sensibility has long persisted of the physical connection that joins body to place.[7] In expressing this bond to the land, people often employ the vocabulary of aesthetics, speaking of the profound effect of the beauty of the landscape or the drama of a view. Or they may express delight in an environment's perceptual qualities—its nuances of color, the movements of light and shadow, the haptic sensation of the breeze, the soughing of the wind. To articulate the powerful aesthetic experience of landscape, writers use the language of engagement when they speak of entering the landscape or of feeling a personal bond with the land or with a place. This is not the hyperbolic speech of rhetoric, for how can it be taken literally if it is not expressed literally? Like the other sensibilities that have atrophied in city dwellers, the feeling of being connected to the land has nearly disappeared in our mobile urban society. That is a deep loss, and it is probably related to the rootlessness and anomie that pervade the unbound mass populations of modern states. Without a somatic attachment to a place, we stand homeless, regardless of our domicile. This bodily awareness of the land often resembles the aesthetic awareness of landscape in being cultivable but largely uncultivated.

Feminist theorists have exposed the invidious gender discrimination inherent in identifying the female body with the earth and the male body with rational distance.[8] It is important to make that case politically, socially, and philosophically, for this gender-based association reflects traditions that devalue both the body and the earth as material and mundane. However, those feminists who revive the ancient traditions of the goddess and invert the gender norm may still preserve the contrast between body wisdom and rational consciousness. Yet why must these be considered exclusive and opposed? And just as its converse is gratuitous, why should valuing the body entail devaluing reflective activity? Not all feminists adjudicate the issue in this way, and other strands in feminist thought suggest a more integrative resolution.

A related development appears in the reawakened interest in pagan practices, challenging the cultural convention that separates humans from nature and makes them its masters. Ceremonies that celebrate the full moon and midsummer, for example, revive ancient rituals that place the body in accord with cosmic events. These mythical and cultural developments, however, often retain divisive philosophical presuppositions that perpetuate the same separation of the body from rational deliberation and nature from human. In celebrating cosmic order, the earth, and the body's bond with their processes, a mystical sense of unity and a blind abandonment to irrational forces sometimes assume romantic proportions, defying reflective thought and unreflective tradition alike. Is it possible to reconcile such diverse domains and restore a harmony that may arguably be considered original? Can we ground human connectedness with the land, with nature, and with the cosmos in a way that does not split the multiple facets of human being into antithetical alternatives?

MERLEAU-PONTY AND THE CONNECTEDNESS OF THE BODY

A philosophy of the body is entangled in even more difficulties than those mentioned at the beginning of this discussion. The very notion of body implies an opposition to subjectivity and raises the need to reconcile the two. How can an inclusive notion of embodiment accommodate the complex levels and orders of consciousness? No ready-made concept expresses the integral whole of human being, and the persistent struggle with the difficulties inherent in subjectivism illustrates how unsatisfactory every attempt to resolve the conflict of consciousness and body has been.

In elaborating ideas of the body, flesh, the chiasm, space, and reversibility, Merleau-Ponty's phenomenological approach to this question sought to overcome the ontological separations that order, or misorder, the human world. Although Merleau-Ponty died before he was able to fully clarify his insights and emancipate philosophical thought from the burden of its divisive history, his emphasis on the body has rich significance for a philosophy of nature that recognizes the interconnectedness of the human and the natural.

Merleau-Ponty's discussion of the flesh offers one way of understanding embodiment, for he explored a notion of flesh that transcends the divisive connotations that hover over the concept of body. In his late, unfinished book *The Visible and the Invisible*, Merleau-Ponty began to develop the idea of a homogeneity of the flesh, a homogeneity that is equally of the world and of my body. Both are made of the same flesh, he claimed, and we can understand the lived body by the flesh of the world.[9] Yet Merleau-Ponty was encumbered by the insistent presence in phenomenology of the baggage of subjectivism. The body both sees and is seen. He wrote: "The flesh of the world is of the Being-seen" at the same time as it is the body as a seeing Being.[10] This dialectic of vision and flesh appears irreconcilable. The flesh of the world is not of the Being-seen but of the Being-seen–Being-seeing, and it is far more than vision. There seems to be a contradiction between vision and flesh, as if Merleau-Ponty were aware of the limitations of vision and wanted to embrace a fleshly whole and yet could not relinquish the Cartesian tradition, with its unbridgeable alienation of self and world. This difficulty is even more problematic when self-awareness originates in the specular self: when the image of myself in the mirror becomes the source of the meaning of my self—an objectification of the self in the interests of a subjectification of the self. The same problem persists if one relinquishes vision for touch, albeit in more materialistic form. Flesh that in touching others touches itself also attempts to use the same perceptual modality as the basis for reconciliation. In so doing, however, it embodies the very division it endeavors to overcome—the separation between touching and the touched.[11]

Conceiving of the body in space offers a different opportunity to develop the kind of reconciliation for which Merleau-Ponty was searching. To speak, as he did, of my body as a charged field suggests that its energy radiates beyond itself to incorporate the world.[12] In writing of the "flesh of the world," Merleau-Ponty used the German word *Einfühlung* to express such an incorporation: "[We] are already *in* the being . . . described, . . . we *are of it*, . . . between it and us there is *Einfühlung*. . . . That means," he continued, "that my body is made of the same flesh as the world (it is a perceived), and moreover that this flesh of my body is shared by the world." But he immediately moved into a play with the dualism between body and world, each encroaching upon the other, transgressing or overlapping each other.[13]

Merleau-Ponty appeared to revert to a naturalistic analogue of the privileged position of idealism when he claimed that "my body is not only one perceived among others, it is the measurant (*measurant*) of all, *Nullpunkt* [zero point] of all the dimensions of the world."[14] This echoes his earlier assertion in "Eye and Mind" that space starts from me "as the zero point or degree zero of spatiality."[15] In *The Visible and the Invisible*, this became the idea that "the perceived world . . . is the ensemble of my body's routes and not a multitude of spatio-temporal individuals."[16] Such a characterization of the body in space creates other difficulties, for although it secures spatial continuity, it does this by establishing at the same time a privileged place for the body. One cannot deny that my body as the place of reference is an inescapable condition of experience. It is the place "from which," but is it inevitably the absolute center, the zero point? Although my body contributes to constituting my being, it is also constituted by other bodies. Nor is my body concrete and delimited; it is rather an approximation, a concentration of being in the midst of activity, not the center of the spatial world. The flesh embodies motion and force but must adapt to the motions and forces of the lived world.

In grappling with the perception of continuity, Merleau-Ponty struggled over this relation of body and world. The perceived world is an extension of the body: "To touch is to touch oneself. . . . Things are the prolongation of my body and my body is the prolongation of the world, through it the world surrounds me."[17] Yet to see the world as the prolongation of my body seems again to regard my body as the zero point. Is not my body just as much a prolongation of the world? Furthermore, both the statement and its converse retain a troublesome dualism. The world does not surround me, for that makes me and the world discrete and different. If my body is continuous with the world, as Merleau-Ponty seems to imply, it doesn't extend out into the world; it is the world, one of its focal points, as are all bodies, in some way. Transcendence of any sort implies separation, and this must be replaced by some kind of continuity. But how is it to be expressed?

Perhaps the distinction between the touching and the touched, which so fascinated Merleau-Ponty, is a duality of language rather than of being. Touching is an assertion of connection, a connectedness that is always present though not always apparent, because it may not be concrete. Can I not touch air? Isn't my body surrounded by an electromagnetic field through which I get "vibes"? Aren't there lines of force that emerge between my self and the objects in proximity to me, between my self and the people in my presence? Am I not always in contact with something, always necessarily touching, whether standing, sitting, lying, or moving? Touch is, in fact, not a duality at all but a contact, literally a "continuity," a holding together. This, indeed, seems to be what Merleau-Ponty was striving toward when he characterized primary perception as a totality we call the world.

> We said that before all philosophy, perception is convinced that it has to do with a confused totality where all things, the bodies and the minds, are together, and which it calls the *world*. . . . Each experiences himself as involved with the others; there is a meeting ground which is Being itself inasmuch as each of us inheres in it through his situation. . . . Each experiences himself given over to a body, to a situation, through them to being, and what he knows of himself passes entirely over to the other the very instant he experiences the other's medusan power. Hence each one knows that he himself and the others are *inscribed* in the world. . . . All that is partial is to be reintegrated.[18]

Attempting to grasp this connection, Merleau-Ponty coined the term *chiasm*. "Chiasm, instead of the For the Other: that means that there is not only a me-other rivalry, but a co-functioning." Later he called this "a me-other exchange," explaining that "we function as one unique body."[19] "Charged field," an expression cited earlier, is a pregnant phrase. It suggests not energy that spreads *out*—for that implies its complement, *in*—but rather energy that pervades the body's locus. The body is a concentration of forces that are part of a larger field—not a *body* but a *self: I am a charged field*.

Yet the concept of chiasm as an intertwining or a reversibility suggests an ambiguity in the close relation between discrete entities and their continuity. Merleau-Ponty was intrigued by the reversibility embedded in the relation between the visible and the seer and between touching and the touched. Each term of the pairs not only depends on but incorporates the other. These are not arbitrary or conventional couplings but congenital ones, so to speak, ontologically bound together.[20] It is an idea embedded in the very "idea of *chiasm*, that is: every relation with being is *simultaneously* a taking and a being taken."[21] Moreover, a similar intimacy is true of the reciprocity of the other senses. The reversibility of audible and hearer is even more suggestive for an ontology of continuity. Here the difference over which Merleau-Ponty labored is still more difficult to keep separate, for unlike the visible and the tactile, there is no perceptual object that stands apart from the experience of hearing, and the interpenetration of hearer and audible is even more striking. Some passages in *The Visible and the Invisible* endeavor to overcome the separations that seem inherent in vision and touch and seek to regain "a world that is neither *one* nor two in the objective sense—which is pre-individual, generality." This is the primal world, "the *antecedent* unity me-world, world and its parts, parts of my body, a unity before segregation, before the multiple dimensions."[22] Here Merleau-Ponty comes close to expressing the idea of continuity as an explicit and vivid metaphysical principle, but he never quite succeeded in emancipating himself from the powerful and insistent dualistic tradition.

BODY-BOUNDARIES AS
CULTURAL PRODUCT

The issue of continuity centers on the question of boundaries and on the nature of that question. Is it a philosophical question, a psychological one, or even a cultural one? Consider the latter: limits of the body that are culturally set. Bodies are not static objects with fixed and permanent boundaries. They are dynamic and fluid, receiving and acting, ingesting and expressing, engaged in a dynamic transaction with the field they inhabit. Every society develops environmental conditions that influence the size and shape of the body's field. The forms these take in contemporary postindustrial societies have parallels in other traditions. Take, for example, the multitude of ways in which people involuntarily receive perceptual stimuli. Visual and auditory events surround us, creating the texture of our environment, yet we have little or no control over most of these events. The very spaces we inhabit are appropriated as a commodity to be as fully exploited as legally allowed. Even the air we breathe in sealed buildings and the smells we encounter in the areas we pass through are not under our control. They are neither chosen nor preferred. These cannot be dismissed as merely "external" events in our perceptual field; they constitute the stimuli we absorb just as we ingest our food, and they become just as much a part of our bodies. Such factors create the perceptual world we inhabit and of which we become a part.

The very forms our bodies take are themselves the product of a cultural environment:

> There are men of the East, he said,
> Who are the East.
> There are men of a province
> Who are that province.
> There are men of a valley
> Who are that valley.
>
> There are men whose words
> Are as natural sounds

Of their places
As the cackle of toucans
In the place of toucans.[23]

Our posture, height and weight, gait, treatment of facial and body hair, skin and outer clothing, and speech, including language, dialect, vocabulary, and grammar—all these are part of the character and quality of our bodily form. Bodily form, moreover, is inseparable from movement, and the setting in which we act leads us to behave in definite ways. The design of objects and spaces provides what Gibson called "affordances for behavior," shapes that draw us on or repel us, leading us to move and act in certain ways.[24] These magnetic features of spaces and objects cast their influence on us as we enter their field of force. To these we must add the well-known cultural influences on the body as the determinant of the self. In postindustrial society, body image has become self-image—the self as appearance. Weight, skin, clothing, manner of speech, and comportment are taken to define the self, to ourselves as much as to others.[25] We inhabit, then, a network of visible and invisible influences ordered by our culture. These form a matrix of forces, an environmental continuum that embraces and directs the body, determining what our bodies, our selves, are.

The body, then, is no simple and discrete physical object, material for the "hard sciences." It is far removed from Descartes' "extension in length, width, and depth," "this mechanism composed of bone and flesh and members, just as it appears in a corpse."[26] Nor is the body a singular object, utterly unique. Body is, rather, a cultural eruption inhabiting a context of conditions, and it includes those dimensions of perception and reflection we hypostatize in reflection as consciousness. The sociologist Chris Shilling characterizes the body as "an unfinished biological and social phenomenon which is transformed, within certain limits, as a result of its entry into, and participation in, society."[27] Norbert Elias described the historical social process by which bodies have become separated and individualized, and Pierre Bourdieu demonstrated how through the social and cultural processes in modern societies the body has become commodified as a form of physical capital.[28] It is meaningful, then, to speak, as Merleau-Ponty does, of the world as flesh and, as the Native Americans do, of the land as my flesh. Yet we must extend world and land to embrace culture: we are the flesh of our cultural world, and the world I inhabit is my flesh. Instead of a physics of the body, then, we have a metaphysics of culture in which we are an embodiment of our cultural environment. How can we characterize this body, this person, in a metaphysics of culture?

By recognizing the interplay of forces that characterize human culture, we are led to acknowledge their powerful influence in shaping the body. Even the contrary view expressed in the dogma of individualism, which has emerged and become increasingly strident in industrial-commercial societies, is itself understood most clearly as a cultural phenomenon. Indeed, we begin to grasp the body, in a metaphysics of culture, not as pure organism, not as an object shaped by social influences, but as fully continuous with the various domains of the human world: the cultural landscape, the predominant modes of technology, and the traditions of food, dress, thought, and behavior. Human culture possesses no absolute divisions or separations but is a fluid whole of interpenetrating processes involving human and material objects, relationships, social interactions, and institutions that coalesce in ever-changing ways. What is in question is not the cultural character of the human body but the modes, forms, and degrees of continuity: social continuity, physical and spatial continuity, temporal continuity. These are what constitute the proper study of humankind.

CONTINUITY AND PLACE

The desire for a congenial integration of body and environment is expressed in the yearning for a sense of place. Increasingly cited as a value that has been lost, place is the home we dream of regaining. Is this merely a romantic fantasy, a nostalgic escape from the hard realities of daily existence in our postindustrial age? I think not. The renewed concern with place is rather a recognition of an undeniable loss, a value whose absence, like the death of a dear friend, is inconsolable. How are we to understand place in a world that is flesh?

We often associate place with a location that has clear identity, one that is benign and congenial, which are qualities we value. Implicit here is a certain mutuality, a reciprocity of person and place, which gives us a sense of belonging. Yet this quality of belonging is more than emotional attachment. Place is the particular landscape we inhabit. It is local and immediate, our lived environment. When fulfilled, it becomes a harmonious unity of body and environment. Place is the world that is my flesh, as Merleau-Ponty would say, a body that I can love as my own.[29] Adrienne Rich calls poetry "an instrument for embodied experience."[30] A landscape, an environment, even more, *is* embodied experience. As such, it is our flesh, our world, our selves. Such an environment is our place, and the more it is fulfilled, the more it is fully ourselves.

This, however, must not be taken as an encomium to an Edenic sense of place that was once lost and is now irrecoverable. Environments are inhospitable, more often than not, and all too frequently they are directly alienating. Such environments are not places we love but prisons from which escape may seem impossible. There is continuity here, too, and the invisible bonds of hostile landscapes are far more tenacious than physical constraints, for we carry them with us wherever we go. Continuity is not the mark of a fulfilling unity of body and environment, for we have as much continuity with hostile environments as with benign ones. The flesh of whatever world I inhabit is my flesh. Continuity is not always positive; indeed, the value we put on a fulfilling sense of place is the correlate of the maleficence of most of the environments we inhabit. Instances of destructive continuity are everywhere, ranging in scope from a bad marriage to a housing project that breeds self-destructive behavior.[31]

Nor does continuity imply a denial of distinctions or differences. The argument for continuity here is an ontological one, not epistemological. Distinctions are necessary, and we constantly make them. The ground for developing distinctions and recognizing differences is pragmatic, and the discriminations we draw in environment change with changing needs and conditions. We readily acknowledge that certain technologies become obsolescent and disappear when they no longer prove useful, as machine production has replaced hand tools. How many cartwrights or wheelwrights still practice their crafts? Similarly, changed conditions elicit changes in behavior patterns. Behind the wheel of a car, the mentality and behavior of a person are transformed, and with little more choice than a worker ant or a gorgonian in a coral reef, a new kind of human emerges. In a similar fashion, distinctions and discriminations change. Consider, for example, the fluid boundaries and widely varying denotation of the concept *man*, when we speak variously of *man* in the political sense or of economic man, of *man* in a religious context or in a philosophical one, of *man* in feminist theory or in the biological sense. And of course, the term changes with different theories within each of these domains. Other ideas, such as *society, wilderness, human being*, and *nature*, vary historically and contextually in similar ways. Mass man is a different creature from a Yankee farmer.

To a large extent, the argument for continuity rests on an awakened sense of experience, on occasions that, though rare, impress us by their vividness and force. Some of these experiences are mystical, some religious. Some are experiences of passion; some have the warmer and more profound qualities of love. But among the most complex and wide-ranging experiences of continuity are those that characterize the deep and powerful aesthetic encounters with art and nature. Continuity epitomizes the fullness of aesthetic engagement. In a way that resembles how we participate in the unfolding of a novel, live in the dynamic elaboration of musical sounds, or enter the landscape of a painting, bodily engagement with environment, when integrated in active perception, becomes aesthetic. And when aesthetic engagement is most intense and complete, it achieves that fulfillment of value we call beauty. An aesthetics of the body is an aesthetics of environment, and the love of the one encompasses the love of the other. This insight, no less philosophical than poetic, Neruda captured in the touching tenderness of "In You the Earth":

Little
rose,
roselet,
at times,
tiny and naked,
it seems
as though you would fit
in one of my hands,
as though I'll clasp you like this
and carry you to my mouth,
but
suddenly
my feet touch your feet and my mouth your lips:
you have grown,
your shoulders rise like two hills,
your breasts wander over my breast,
my arm scarcely manages to encircle the thin
new-moon line of your waist:
in love you have loosened yourself like sea water:
I can scarcely measure the sky's most spacious eyes
and I lean down to your mouth to kiss the earth.[32]

Aesthetic appreciation, like all experience, is an engagement of the body, a body aesthetic that strives to extend and realize the possibilities of perception and meaning. An aesthetically fulfilling environment is one with which we achieve those possibilities.

◆ CHAPTER SEVEN ◆

Architecture and the Aesthetics of Continuity

ARCHITECTURAL TRADITION AND CHANGE

Although architecture has long been practiced as an art, its acceptance as a fine art was confirmed only in the eighteenth century, when the modern classification of the arts was finally decided.[1] This was the same period in which modern aesthetics assumed its definitive form. Architecture was thus absorbed into the august body of the "fine" arts and was explained by the theory of art—the theory of *those* arts.

In many respects, architecture is a paradigm of art in the traditional sense. It offers singular objects of striking size and appearance that stand apart and dominate their surroundings. Such structures are often awe-inspiring, and their reverential power is transferred by association to the individuals and institutions identified with them. As an ideal and in practice, the tradition that honors monumentality and constructs edifices is what the popular mind associates with architecture, and this tradition continues to supply the paradigm to critics and scholars. Magnificence and power are taken to be the body and meaning of this art.

Such a model continues to serve us. Structures have grown more lofty and massive. Government buildings, becoming ever larger, continue the classical tradition of solid monumentality, and office towers have long since surpassed cathedrals in size and height. Unlike medieval cathedrals, which were squeezed in by neighboring shops and houses, skyscrapers often stand in grand isolation in their own plazas. And as their size and implicit power have grown, so has the homage they inspire. Such buildings, vying with one another for supremacy of mass and height, represent the continuing tradition of architecture as edifice.

Yet architecture has also assimilated many other currents of style, thought, and role. Even as the traditional model has continued to have theoretical and practical influence, a succession of new forces has emerged. As the twentieth century nears its end, these have intensified into a confusion of possibilities, including modernism and postmodernism, deconstruction, neostructuralism, the rediscovery of ethnic traditions, and other trends as yet unnamed. Architectural practice has also moved away from monumentality to encompass less imposing structures such as the apartment complex and the shopping plaza. The perimeter of architecture has expanded beyond separate buildings to embrace urban groupings, such as the cultural center and the pedestrian mall. And it has enlarged its scope still farther, redeveloping urban zones into "cities" that incorporate apartments, offices, shops, schools, and parks. Moreover, the range of architecture has moved in a contrary direction to accept a structure that was once considered too lowly to be allowed into the elevated domain of grand art—the private dwelling. Domestic architecture has become an important genre, providing an opportunity to display new theories and innovative designs.

Along with expansive forces, integrative ones have been at work. We have become more aware of the physical and social context of a building, of the relation of its height, mass, and facade to nearby structures. Physical connections have begun to appear, too, such as second-story walkways that join buildings above the street level and provide enclosed pedestrian pathways, binding separate structures and independent businesses into a network, an urban complex. This is also a sign of the increasing recognition of architecture's social role and function. Could we be moving, in the manner of Soleri's arcologies, toward total, integrated urban structures?

Such a multiplicity of tendencies reflects the present ambiguity of architectural art and, at the same time, our own equivocal position in its historical process. Perhaps we are caught in the decline and dissipation of an exhausted tradition. Perhaps we are trapped between the solutions of an irrelevant past and the irresolutions of an indeterminate future. Possibly we stand at the brink of a new view of the human world. These confusing directions offer an opportunity to reconsider the axiomatic principles of architectural theory, in particular, to articulate certain theoretical assumptions behind the expansive and integrative impulses in contemporary architecture. By stating what may have been felt only implicitly, we may discover both a key and a guide to the transformation of architecture and, as a consequence, of our entire built world.

INTEGRATING DISTINCTIONS
AND OPPOSITIONS

The usual practice of critical inquiry is to develop distinctions and to comment on relationships among the factors that have been identified. Discussions of the arts typically note differences and draw contrasts, and this is particularly true in architectural theory and criticism. Like other distinctions, those in architecture tend to be expressed as oppositions: the facade is contrasted with the interior, the building with its site, architectural design with landscape design, decoration with utility, form with function, built areas with natural ones, and, the source of many of these distinctions, human needs and desires with natural processes. Architectural success is often measured by the ability to balance such opposing values and combine these dissonances into a harmonious whole.

Let us instead set this critical discussion in another direction, not discerning differences and opposing alternatives but identifying resemblances and developing continuities. That will make it easier to recognize the interrelations of various architectural factors and the interdependence of architecture with society and environment. It would be useful, for example, to reconsider the contrasts just cited by positioning them as distant points of a continuum, so that their resemblances and connections begin to emerge in place of the conceptual order of oppositions. A facade, for example, can set the tone for the decorative features, forms, and spaces of the interior, instead of being taken merely as a shell preserved for historical or other external reasons, a coating calculated to evoke associations of reverence, tradition, or scientific progress, or merely as a sensuous surface. And there are ways of merging the interior with what is beyond it by using glass walls, extending the roof or the floor plane, furnishing enclosed spaces with planters that bring the vegetation indoors, or using a form that embraces its site.

We can even discard the time-honored opposition of utility and beauty by recognizing that it is embedded in an aesthetic that rests more on philosophical history than on architectural experience. The contemplative aesthetics of the eighteenth century codified the classical distinction between theoretical and practical knowledge into a separation of beauty and use, the latter bound up with purpose, the former independent of utility. Architectural theory echoed that division by keeping structural demands entirely apart from aesthetic considerations. One response to this isolation of beauty from practice has been to think that function alone automatically achieves beauty of a kind. Sometimes, as in brutalism, it led to the assumption that directly reflecting the materials and structure of a building would ensure its aesthetic value. The division of beauty and use, or the assimilation of the aesthetic to the practical, seems rather naive now, the triumph of a technological mentality more simple in conception than satisfactory in execution. Indeed, both brutalism and its decorative contrary, Beaux Arts architecture, implicitly accept the ideal of a universal standard, itself a pillar of traditional aesthetics and exemplified most powerfully in this century by the international style. Many of these ideas and movements stand at different points in the modernist tradition, which is itself a direct outgrowth of the eighteenth-century aesthetic.

A growing force in the twentieth century, however, has been the recognition of different ways in which beauty and use are inseparable. One of these lies in the unity of the practical and the aesthetic that is typical of vernacular architecture. Another is a new awareness of the beauty inherent in finely crafted objects of practical function, whether they are the product of a long cultural tradition or the deliberate accomplishment of a modern artisan. The influence of a craft aesthetic appears in the designs of Mies van der Rohe, I. M. Pei, and Fumihiko Maki; in the writings of Christopher Alexander; and in the work of others influenced by these figures.[2]

Another distinction that is beginning to be displaced is that between a building and its site. The concept seems obvious enough, but it has taken architects a long time to recognize the site-specific nature of good architecture. The history of architecture holds outstanding examples of this, but only recently has it come to be broadly recognized as a general precept. Two early modern architects who realized the intimate relation of building and site were Frank Lloyd Wright and Julia Morgan. Wright is well known for his sensitive application of this principle, and Morgan was a nineteenth-century American architect whose Asilomar Conference Center on the California coast blends its buildings with an uneven site populated by high pines. Standardized designs that have been imposed thoughtlessly on the landscape, from the rectangular block skyscraper to the ubiquitous ranch house, are being replaced by more imaginative and complex shapes that echo landforms and regional traditions, by embellishment that uses historical and regional motifs, and by local building materials that mirror the land.

The sensitivity of architecture to site is a powerful integrative force. It recognizes that a building is not self-sufficient or self-contained but both influences and is influenced by what surrounds it. Ways of joining structure and site include using indigenous species for foundation plantings and other landscaping, and emulating not only the physical and geological aspects of the location but also the buildings that stand nearby. We can extend the reciprocity of building and site to the neighborhood, to pedestrian and vehicular patterns, and eventually to the entire built complex of which the individual building is a constituent. When a building is not related to its physical and social context, the effects may vary from indifference to alienation and even outright hostility.

Underlying many of these customary oppositions is a difficulty in grasping the relation that human beings have to the natural world. Whereas indigenous peoples develop architectural forms and other cultural adaptations that reflect the connections, indeed the continuities, of their activities with natural forces, many intellectual, religious, and cultural traditions have found profound discord. A separation of some sort between nature and what is distinctively human—a separation sometimes sharp enough to be seen as a conflict—developed in Hindu and Christian doctrine and in much of classical Greek and Hellenistic philosophy. The beliefs and practices that developed from these doctrines inherited this acquired characteristic. Moreover, this separation of the human and the natural has combined with modern science and technology and with the ever-increasing commercialism of an industrializing world to become a dominant feature of the contemporary scene. Yet this attitude is beginning to shift. Recent social and political movements, particularly the environmental movement, are rethinking conventional beliefs and values and working to reconcile this opposition of human and natural worlds. These are important signs of a change in the prevailing view. The conflict between these alternative ways of understanding the relationship of human and environmental interests will likely increase as we recognize more vividly how the environmental effects of our actions in turn affect ourselves.

From a larger perspective, however, we can see these separations as an aberrant development in the history of human habitation. For most of that history, an intimacy existed between humans and the natural world. People acted in and on their environment with care and respect. A dependence on natural factors led them to proceed not from a sense of power over an alien world but from an awareness of harmony with a place that was part of themselves. Alternative traditions and ideas reflected this sensibility. Taoism, Zen Buddhism, and natural theology are religions that bind people to nature. The pre-Socratics, Spinoza, Schelling, Emerson, Thoreau, and Dewey are philosophical thinkers for whom this connection is basic. In the latter part of the nineteenth century and throughout the twentieth, philosophic movements such as positivism, evolutionism, naturalism, and pragmatism sought to embody a similar insight. The endeavor to reintegrate human and nature has become increasingly influential.

What is most significant about the instances of separation and opposition mentioned earlier is that such divisions are neither given nor necessary. Conceptualizing the human world through connections and continuities offers an alternative and leads to a different paradigm for architecture, one of relatedness and unity. Can we extend this model to other, still broader contexts and relationships?

THE ARCHITECTURE OF
CITY AND ENVIRONMENT

The conventional distinction between architecture and the city is clear enough: architecture concerns the design of individual structures, whereas the city is the coherent collection of such structures. Even though such a distinction may appear obvious, the resemblance between architecture and the city is striking. The same concepts of mass, space, and volume help order the configurations of both. Both respond to considerations of human movement and use, and both offer a qualitative environment of surfaces, textures, colors, and light that affect not only our visual sensibility but also our tactile and especially kinesthetic awareness. Architecture and city not only display parallels; they cannot be kept apart. If the aesthetic of a building can be extended to include its site, its site is affected by contiguous sites, just as a structure cannot usually be regarded in isolation but is apprehended in relation to its neighbors. Indeed, as we expand the range of our perception, the building becomes part of an entire district, and this, in turn, of the city.

Architectural experience, then, is a microcosm of urban experience. The perception, the dynamics, the function of architecture are all mirrored in the larger built environment we call the city. And in reciprocal fashion, we can grasp urban experience as architecture "writ large." Streets are urban corridors, gateways are doors, plazas are urban rooms for social intercourse, and houses are areas reserved for private activity. Our customary practices affect the temperature, the air, the very climate of a city, just as they do the atmosphere of a home or a building. It could be argued that the most representative architectural form of the collective mass culture of the postindustrial age is the city. This is the quintessential human landscape, and the same basic principles of coherence and context apply here as to an individual structure. Although the scale is vastly greater and there are emergent qualities in a city that a building does not possess, the central concepts are remarkably alike and the dynamic of their function very much the same. In fact, as buildings become more cohesive and their structures more contiguous, the line between city and building will be hard to locate and may eventually disappear.

Does the city define the limit of the built environment, or can the connections, the continuity of building and city be carried further? What about the city's place in the landscape? Isn't the city a part of the region in which it is situated in more than a geographical sense? These are interesting questions for an aesthetics of continuity. Let us consider them in two ways: first by exploring the parallels between the city and the larger landscape, and then by examining their connections and boundaries.

It is curious how far one can go in applying architectural features to the landscape. If imagination is given some license, we can see the landscape as exhibiting a surprising number of architecture-like elements. Roads are corridors; turnoffs and drives are entrances and exits. Fields, meadows, and glades—whether bounded by stone walls, fences, hedges, or ditches or merely by texture, contents, or function—are rooms in the landscape and, like rooms, possess as much character as their owner or other influences may give them. We often speak of the height of the cloud cover as a ceiling, and a break in the clouds through which sunlight streams can be seen as a celestial skylight. The ground becomes a floor, a trail through dense growth a hallway; a mounting path resembles a stairway, an overlook a balcony, the swerve of a grassy bank an amphitheater, a border of trees a wall, and the concave curve of the sky a dome. It is remarkable how often we metaphorically assign the names of building elements to features of the landscape, and the parallel can as easily be drawn in the reverse direction. Sunken living rooms, for example, emulate the protective hollow or valley, as the groins in the vaulting of cathedral ceilings mirror the canopy of branches in a grove. One could construct a veritable homology between architecture and landscape.

How does it change our perception of an environment to recognize its similarities to a house or a building? How does it change our perception of a building to regard it not in opposition to environment but in imitation of it? As our understanding widens here,

so perhaps does our perception, until we may dwell in the landscape, as Heidegger would have it, and see our home as a landscape
and the landscape as our home.

Beyond the architecture of environment, there are other connections between city and landscape that transgress old boundaries. The sharp lines and distinct colors on a map that define the
extent of cities are as insubstantial as the walls that once bounded
medieval cities are today. The first are cartographic fictions; the
second survive mostly as historical curiosities. We can no longer
clearly identify the physical perimeter of a city. It spreads out from
its center with decreasing density, until commercial and industrial
pockets and corridors merge with agricultural areas or uncultivated terrain. Metropolitan spread has absorbed vast regions of
the eastern and western seaboards of the United States. Where
cities once had protective boundaries, there is now neither boundary nor protection.

It is well to remember that just as the concept of a landscape is
a human construct, the landscape as a geographical area is a
human construction. Our actions have not only shaped inhabited
landscapes but also irreparably changed those that are no longer
and perhaps never were inhabited. During the same time that the
wilderness lost its fearful mystery and awe (that is, by the latter
part of the eighteenth century) the industrial domination of the
landscape began in earnest, and the idea of primeval wilderness
became a literary fiction.[3] "Knowledge is power," Francis Bacon
had proclaimed at the beginning of modern science. Scientific
knowledge meant power over nature, and the impulse to impose
the one's will—so characteristic of half-civilized individuals and
societies—was partially sublimated into the domination of nature.
But the battle takes subtler form here in the landscape, and the
consequences are delayed and indirect. As in so many other cases
of conflict, the opposition of human and nature is not clearly drawn,
and their forces not separable. Nature is not out there, a place apart
from us. We have, instead, a continuity of humans and natural
world. What we need now is to reconceptualize our world in a way
that comes to terms with this, for what we do in environment we
do to ourselves—to the same air we breathe into our bloodstreams,

to the same water that is the liquid of our lives, to the same earth whose fruits become our bodies.

THE EARTH IS MY BODY

We can now see the fallacy in architecture's conventional wisdom that "the ultimate task of architecture is to act in favor of man: to interpose itself between man and the natural environment in which he finds himself."[4] This seemingly incontrovertible axiom, which James Marston Fitch took as the fundamental thesis of his major study of American architecture, is especially surprising for a commentator whose sensitivity to the experiential factor in architecture was exemplary.[5] Yet it testifies to the deep-rooted strength of the belief. Now, however, we can rephrase the mission of architecture by transposing that axiom onto a new plane: the ultimate task of architecture is to act in favor of the human environment by mediating the reciprocity of people and the landscape that is their natural home. This is a far more complex task than designing shelters against the wilderness, a far more sophisticated undertaking than building edifices. The architect must now go beyond being alternately a materials and structural engineer, a designer, and even an applied artist. Perhaps we should return to the medieval practice of architecture as a collective art and employ the expert services of the ecologist, the environmental psychologist, the cultural geographer, the anthropologist, the landscape architect, the urban and regional planner, the environmental artist, and the aesthetician, in addition to the engineer, the designer, and the architect.

Instead of an opposition between human and nature, then, we must grasp their continuity. Instead of architecture imposing itself on the landscape or even responding to the landscape, perhaps we can invert the order and encourage architects to take environment as their model. Their task would then be to fashion structures that do not interpose themselves between humans and the natural environment, that do not even mediate between them, but that respond to and articulate the continuities that bind people to their landscape, a landscape that makes them human—a humanized landscape, a naturalized humanity.

For our culture of opposition, aggression, and defensiveness, this is a difficult task. It is understandable how sensitive commentators, presented with this scene, look to architecture for protection. Bachelard, the poet of space, regarded the house as "a tool for analysis of the human soul. . . . Our soul is an abode. And by remembering 'houses' and 'rooms,' we learn to 'abide' in ourselves."[6] Although houses and rooms do possess an intimate bond with ourselves, Bachelard saw the self as subjectivity, and this led him to subjectify space and to an aesthetics of withdrawal. Yet we find ourselves intimately connected to the rooms and houses we inhabit precisely because we cannot separate our selves from them. We see ourselves in the houses of our childhood; they contribute to the selves that we are; we become ourselves *in* and *through* those places. Here, in the heart of withdrawal, is the very continuity, that fusion of self and place, of which I have been speaking. That fusion, however, does not end at the outside wall. Even Levinas, who, like Bachelard, accepted a division of inner and outer and regarded the home as an inwardness, an interiority, also recognized that it borders on an exteriority. The private domain of one's being opens out to the world. Yet we now see an alternative to this defense of the self by separation and insulation. We must move beyond the architecture of refuge to an architecture of continuity.

The special accomplishment of writers whose work centers on particular regions lies not just in their ability to convey a sense of the character and distinctiveness of these areas but also in their ability to locate human identity in them. What they impart has more than autobiographical interest. The appeal is universal, for it exemplifies how a person is formed in the human and natural landscape. We learn from Wendell Berry's essays on Kentucky, Barry Lopez's travels in the Arctic and the desert, and Ivan Doig's reminiscences of Montana about a kind of connection with landscape that we know in our bones but have not articulated, an inheritance more direct and more powerful than anything genetic.[7] Writers like these help us discover a sense of home that is often obscured by the impersonality of mass culture and standardized architecture, a home that is the fusion of person and place. If our obsession were more with places than with genes, we might be more successful in discovering who we are in where we are.

We come by various routes, then, to an overarching union of people, architecture, and landscape. Connections hold, not divisions; continuities, not separations. The architectural structure is bonded, on the one hand, to its inhabitants and, on the other, to its site, neighborhood, town or city, and region, and eventually, by influences that range from the climatic to the cosmic, to the universe. This is the ultimate integration of the architectural and the human: in continuity lies identity.

CHAPTER EIGHT

Education as Aesthetic

In his essay "The Aims of Education," written more than half a century ago, Alfred North Whitehead enunciated an ideal that can stand as an exemplary statement for us today: "What education has to impart is an intimate sense for the power of ideas, for the beauty of ideas, and for the structure of ideas, together with a particular body of knowledge which has peculiar reference to the life of the being possessing it."[1] Enlightened as this statement is, it is not the first expression of such an educational aim. We know well that if we whet the student's interest, get her involved, and create an active fascination with what he is learning, the student will learn not only more but better, and with greater effect. The irony is all the sadder when we find ourselves falling far short of achieving the condition that Whitehead wrote about so forcefully. But what is the condition Whitehead described as "being alive with living thoughts?"[2] By what signs can it be known? How can it be described? Perhaps if we could offer some specific answers to these questions we would be able to select those methods that would help bring it about.

What strikes me most about this condition of being alive with living thoughts is the resemblance it has to descriptions that have been given of our experiences of art. In *Science and the Modern World*, Whitehead himself suggests such a connection: "When you understand all about the sun and all about the atmosphere and all about the rotation of the earth, you may still miss the radiance of the sunset. There is no substitute for the direct perception of the concrete achievement of a thing in its actuality. We want concrete fact with a high light thrown on what is relevant to its preciousness. What I mean is art and aesthetic education. . . . What we want is to draw out habits of aesthetic apprehension."[3] This has a curious parallel in the common refrain of many contemporary artists that we must join art with life.

One might say that this is all well and good, but education is concerned with knowledge, whereas art, especially in its present orgy of exaggerated sensibility, is violently anti-intellectual. White-head can set us right again. "Culture," he begins his essay, "is activity of thought, and receptiveness to beauty and humane feeling. Scraps of information have nothing to do with it."[4] Here we have a clue to the bond that unites art and education: they are joined with the cement of culture.

Pursuing the suggestive parallel between the aesthetic process and the educational one will help illuminate this idea of the contribution of aesthetic education to the larger culture. Through this analogy, we may discover some rather surprising and suggestive implications. I shall proceed in three stages. First I examine the participating elements of the aesthetic process and make some observations on the perceptual qualities of the field in which this process works. Next I apply a similar analysis to the educational process and comment on the experiential characteristics of inquiry that are aesthetic. And finally I ask whether such education can serve as part of a larger social environment, one that achieves an aesthetic character. Let me begin with the experience of art.

THE AESTHETIC PROCESS

If we probe the situation in which we characteristically experience art, we find four basic contributing factors.[5] There is an art object, such as a painting, a musical work, a dance, or a poem. Each of these has a set of perceptual features that it shares in some way with other objects of the same art but that take unique form in every particular work. The arrangement of color, line, light and shadow, space; the combination of sounds, rhythm, motion; the patterned sequence of bodily movements; the choice and order of word patterns and verbal images—in each art object such elements occur in distinctive ways. The activity of appreciating it involves capturing with an acute awareness how these particular qualities and features move and develop.

Of course, no art object springs spontaneously into existence. Part of its claim to an aesthetic role lies in its parentage. Every object of art is the work of an artist, and we orphan it by overlooking this fact. This is not to say that we should become distracted by biography, psychology, politics, religion, or any of the other fascinating but perceptually unimportant regions into which the genesis of an art object can lead. Rather, the object must be seen as the product of an activity, since it is fashioned through the skillful manipulation of perceptual materials, guided by choice, impulse, happy accident, and an originating awareness. To the trained eye it shows the signs of its birth, not just in the brush strokes or in a comparison of different versions, but far more importantly through the creative act of perception that must be lived through in experiencing it. By participating in this creative process we relive the course of the original perception.

This introduces a third element into the aesthetic field, the appreciative observer. That role is not a passive one of merely responding to the stimuli generated by the object of art. In the experience of art we engage the object intensely, re-creating with our own capacities and experiences a process that parallels the artist's original one. Here is where the traditional accounts of appreciation are so misleading. Burdened with a cognitive model of awareness, laboring under a history of denying the sensory richness of experience, deflected by a tradition of aristocratic diffidence that demeans the artistic process as the labor of an artisan, in sharp contrast to the superior contemplation of a removed, rational observer, the act of appreciation has been regarded as the disinterested attention to an object isolated from its setting. Illusion by means of interjecting a kind of psychological distance has become the watchword of aesthetic contemplation. In our experiences of art, however, although not yet in our theory, this misleading attitude is happily fading away. And this is due in no small measure to the insistence of modern art that we actively engage the art object.

Finally, equal attention must be given to the factor of performance. It is important to realize that, in a significant sense, all the arts are performing arts. A performer is not merely an agent who transmits the inspiration (or, if one is more prosaic, realizes the notation) of a composer or choreographer to an audience. In arts such as music, dance, and theater, the performer activates the art object, bringing it into perceptual play. Yet in the other arts, as well, the appreciator performs the same function in the dynamic of the appreciative process, realizing the aesthetic potential of the painting, the film, or the poem through active perception.

One more point must be made here: the object, artist, appreciator, and performer need not be separate, independent individuals or elements that come together in the activity of art. These are rather distinguishable facets of an experiential unity, bound together in mutual tension. Each aspect functions and achieves its identity as it joins with the others on an aesthetic occasion. One can use the same framework to describe appreciating objects of natural beauty, where the artistic function is taken over by the activity of nature, or appreciating manufactured objects, where the mass-produced article has its genesis not in the work of an individual craftsperson but in the designer's conception and the manufacturing process. What I have identified in this analysis as four factors is but one in aesthetic experience.

An important difference holds between analysis and experience in aesthetics. Analysis is for the future or perhaps the past; the only aesthetic reality lies in the continuum of a present. Commonly we confound the disparate acts of analysis and perception, taking the conceptual object as if it were the only one and overlooking the perceptual object. If we keep these processes distinct, we notice that the perceptual qualities of the aesthetic field are of a quite different order from the structural elements into which it can be divided. This is similar, in the philosophy of science, to the distinction between the logic of discovery and the logic of justification. What is striking about aesthetic perception is its qualitative directness and immediacy. The experience is sharply intuitive; a glow of perceptual awareness emanates from the catalytic combination of factors, enriched by the resonance of background and experience that each person brings to the situation. These factors fuse into a complex unity of perception that is unique to that experience, with its own distinctive intrinsic qualities.

Two features of aesthetic perception have special interest here. The first has to do with the inner dynamic of the aesthetic field. The direct perceptual force of aesthetic experience carries its own authenticity. The hard realism of the factual world has not yet been achieved, and questions of truth and accuracy do not arise. "Things . . . are what they are experienced as," wrote John Dewey. "We have a contrast, not between a Reality, and various approximations to, or phenomenal representations of Reality, but between different reals of experience."[6] Dewey's postulate of immediate empiricism is a remarkably apt characterization of the perceptual condition of the aesthetic field. Whatever is experienced aesthetically is real as it is experienced. All perceptual qualities are equally authentic, since perception without judgment cannot be in error. There is no distinction between illusion and reality, dream and actuality. In the realm of art, everything is perceptually equal; thus the criterion of artistic success must lie within the field, not outside it.[7]

The second feature of aesthetic perception that bears noting concerns the quality of the time and space in which language functions in art. As a medium of direct apprehension, words are not the hardened receptacles of dead meanings that have been gathered from the rich ground of vital experience. Poetic language—that is, the creative use of words in any literary genre—achieves the imaginative reality of living thoughts. "Thus speech, in the speaker," wrote Merleau-Ponty, "does not translate ready-made thought, but accomplishes it." In aesthetic expression, "the process of expression brings the meaning into being or makes it effective, and does not merely translate it. . . . Thought and expression . . . are simultaneously constituted. . . . The spoken word is a genuine gesture, and it contains its meaning in the same way as the gesture contains its. This is what makes communication possible."[8] Put somewhat differently, poetic language functions as image rather than as metaphor, to use Bachelard's distinction; that is, it functions as the direct perception of an image and not as the conscious analogy by which one understands a metaphor.[9] This is a far cry from the dull prose of most discourse, where language is a meaningless pastiche of clichés and formulas whose once living meanings are lost beneath the wrappings of habit and convention.

THE AESTHETIC FIELD IN EDUCATION

This account of the aesthetic field is intended as a descriptive analysis of the participating factors and perceptual characteristics of aesthetic experience. It finds a surprising degree of confirmation in both the psychology of perception and the observations of experienced observers who approach the aesthetic situation open to what actually happens. Moreover, the aesthetic field offers an especially apt account of the experience of the contemporary arts, in which the interplay of factors in the aesthetic situation is often particularly pronounced.[10] Further, this description is effective in explaining away many of the puzzles that have dogged the history of aesthetics and in opening up aspects of aesthetic perception that have been overlooked or ignored. What is particularly interesting are the suggestive implications of applying this account of the aesthetic field to a social situation, particularly the setting in which education takes place. Let us explore some of the consequences.

Each of the four factors participating in the aesthetic field has an analogue in the educational situation. The art object corresponds with the subject matter or project that is the center of attention, the particular topic being developed or problem being explored. The artist, whose work produces an object that participates as the focus of aesthetic perception, corresponds with the scientist or the scholar. This person is the originating contributor in the knowledge process, who may bring fresh ideas and revealing insights to the search for widened understanding. Through the working procedures of the discipline or the operations demanded by the problem, the scholar-scientist adds to the range of knowledge and our depth of understanding. The appreciator in the aesthetic field corresponds with the student who attends to the subject under consideration with an active interest, involved and absorbed much as one becomes engrossed in a musical performance or a novel. When a student is actively engaged in what is going on, a transformation occurs in the perception of space and time that resembles what happens in art: space expands to encompass the imaginary realm, and time is lifted out of the ordinary chronological sequence into the order of the work. Finally, the performer in art corresponds with the teacher, who shares the similar function of activating the object of attention, opening up the subject to awareness, engaging the student in it, and bringing it to life in mutual realization. Like the artistic performer, the teacher is sometimes dispensable, and that role is then filled by the student. Indeed, the entire point of the teacher's art, at least as it relates to the student's interest, is to become unnecessary. And just as the aesthetic field is a physical-perceptual whole, so the educational field is a vital unity of teacher, student, scholar, and subject. In the perceptual field of successful educational experience, these four are not independent elements cast in various combinations. They are rather facets of a single total activity, and the educational field is the plane of experience on which all these facets converge.

As the aesthetic field has its own perceptual authenticity in which everything is equally real and the criterion of success is internal, so the educational field has a self-sufficiency of its own. We are far too grade- or goal-oriented in how we conceive and direct the educational encounter, and this discourages an interest in the subject matter at hand and a delight in working with it. The pattern of inquiry has its own justification, for it is concerned primarily with solving a problem or dispelling confusion. Its purpose lies, then, in working through its issue or problem in a way that is true to the project and leads to its resolution or fulfillment. Thus the educational process, as educational, is essentially noncompetitive, for a competitive activity finds its success in displacing others, not in productive accomplishment, and this is entirely foreign to the cognitive achievement that distinguishes successful inquiry. In an aesthetically guided educational situation, correspondence with an external standard of measurement is relinquished in favor of achieving the resolution of the problem or the illumination of understanding.

Like the aesthetic process, the educational field possesses a creative dynamic of its own. This is far from the mechanical routine of rote learning, drill, and unthinking repetition and memorization. In a vital educational process there is genuine creativity at work. Ideas are pondered as if for the first time, expressed, manipulated, and rendered in language that has a living quality, like that of the poetic image. To formulate a thought in one's own language is to give birth to it; it may be a rebirth, but only in historical perspective, for an idea first seized upon and learned has an original quality. If it fits into place and has significance for a student's interests, it has vitality. To ask a student to apply it or to find examples is to ask him or her to explore the unknown and see what can be discovered. Writing, similarly, possesses its own creative character. It demands that ideas be codified in language, sharpened and structured into stable grammatical form. Working ideas out and exploring their relationships on a chalkboard is publicly creative, and doing it in cooperation with other students becomes a social act of creation. Words here are not the dull and lifeless matter of routine repetition but have the breath of living language. This is far removed from that "celibacy of the intellect which is divorced from the concrete contemplation of the complete fact," with which Whitehead thought the modern world had replaced the celibacy of the medieval learned class.[11] A similar poverty of language lies in the triumph of the engineering mentality, where technical jargon becomes a substitute for literacy. Genuine educational experience involves working with thought as a creative activity.

Thus the successful educational situation has a remarkable resemblance to the aesthetic field. Although this description may appear unfamiliar, it is not intended as an account of the usual teaching situation but as a descriptive analysis of the educational process when it is vital and creative. Most teachers and students have experienced this, but the pity lies in its rarity. Yet understanding something about the aesthetics of education can aid us in cultivating such qualities.[12]

EDUCATION AND ENVIRONMENT

This parallel that education has with the aesthetic situation has important implications for pedagogical practice, yet it also stands as an exemplification of a different sort. Just as we can use the model of the aesthetic field to illuminate the educational process, so we can use the educational aesthetic synecdochically as an exemplar of the social one, for as education can follow an aesthetic model, so too can the social process, more generally. In this way, the educational situation can be seen as a model of a social environment, a social order that is at the same time an aesthetic order. The fulfillment that is found in the process itself, rather than exclusively in the goal, the heightened awareness in the perceptual immediacy of the situation, the encouragement of insight, a dynamic generated through internal momentum instead of external pressures, creative development rather than mechanical repetition—all these mark both a fulfilling social process and an aesthetic one.

The twentieth century has seen some relaxation of formal and authoritarian structures in education, a change facilitated by physical changes in the design of classrooms and school buildings. We now recognize the close connection between the design of the learning environment and the kind of learning, both formal and informal, that goes on. We have discovered that such factors as the seating arrangement, the wall colors and floor covering, and the kind of light and its source have a substantial influence on the educational process. Both setting and process join in constituting the environment of education, at times an aesthetic environment. Cannot this exemplify in miniature the possibilities of the larger social process?

Designing an aesthetic environment, whether for education or for some other social situation, is not a euphemism for a subtle form of social control. In our age, the control of populations, by either direct force or indirect manipulation, has reached a virtuoso level of scope and power. The pervasive and powerful influence of the designed environment, which virtually everyone inhabits nearly all the time, is inescapable. At work or at home, as consumers or as voters, during recreation or entertainment, worshipping or socializing, the settings in which we carry on our activities have been shaped for those uses. Most are designed for control, directing our physical movements, our choices, at times our very beliefs. Nondirective environments are rare, for we tend to perpetuate those other old and familiar patterns, even in our families and voluntary social groups. Although there are some notable exceptions, these are not common. Like a hierarchical social structure, the directed environment is nearly impossible to avoid. In an aesthetic social environment, however, hierarchy and control have no place.

That is why the aesthetic model is so important here. It offers an alternative, one that embodies many of the features we associate with a genuinely democratic ethos: welcoming difference, valuing individuality, recognizing the importance of the activity as well as the goal. These very characteristics, curiously enough, bear the mark of the aesthetic process, and we can design environments that encourage these traits. I choose the word *encourage* deliberately, for openness is embedded in aesthetic experience.

The social environment, then, like the physical environment from which it cannot be separated, may take on a pervasive aesthetic character. We have intimations of this in some classrooms—those rare but unforgettable times in our personal past. Other, similar social environments may appear—in sport, in camaraderie, in friendship, in love, in worship. Can this aesthetic integration, this aesthetic unity in a social situation, stand as an exemplar of the larger social order?

CHAPTER NINE

Aesthetics and Community

POLITICAL SCIENCE AND SOCIAL ORDER

Political science and political theory have a parallel appeal for understanding human society, the one presumably grounded on fact, the other on ideas. "Presumably" is an essential qualifier here, since, as in religious and moral thought, it is especially difficult to separate facts from ideas, and to separate both of these from ideological presuppositions. Political theory and political science, moreover, can be said to have had a parallel origin in Western thought, the first in Plato's writings on the state, in which the idea of practice was never absent, and the second in the political philosophy of Aristotle, which combined classification and judgment with its descriptions. This tells us something about the complementarity, perhaps the inseparability, of theory and science.

Yet neither political science nor theory entirely satisfies our desire to understand the structure and workings of human society. This is so partly because the forms and conditions of societies have varied as widely as the judgments of their success, and generalization is precarious. Moreover, dissatisfaction and disapproval, from within the social order and without, regularly lead to efforts at change in historical societies, some of them transformative. Given such discontent, it is little wonder that since classical times philosophers and political theorists have attempted to envision what a truly satisfactory human order would be like, a moral order, a state of social fulfillment. Sometimes these proposals have been ameliorative, sometimes utopian, often provocative.

The usual approach to understanding social order is a political one: classification by governmental form, by the pattern in which power is distributed. Hence the common contrast of such forms as monarchy, aristocracy, oligarchy, republic, democracy, and state communism. But political order is not the most basic level of analysis. It rests on several assumptions—about what people are like, including beliefs about human nature and, indeed, that there is such a thing as human nature; about people's motives and goals; about power as an isolable quantity; and about the nature of society. In contrast, I want to propose a somewhat novel ordering of communities, one based on the character and quality of human relations, on the nature of social experience. Although social experience is neither simple in structure nor quantifiable, it has the virtue of being directly accessible to the participants and so, in one form or another, to everyone. And it can be described in useful ways both literally, to a degree, and figuratively.

The discussion that follows, although limited, endeavors to make a significant statement about community. After some observations about individual and community—surely the central factors in social philosophy—I offer a convenient schema within which to place many of the endlessly varied instances of human association. This is not an exercise in typology, for the rational, the moral, and the aesthetic communities—the forms I use—are neither pure nor logically exclusive. They do, however, distinguish different kinds of social experience and understanding, and they are useful for grouping actually existing societies. Most important, they represent real alternatives in social choice. Since moral criteria underlie every conception of community, and since normative experience is the basis on which we eventually come to evaluate social forms, let me begin with some observations about ethics.

ETHICAL INDIVIDUALISM
AND HUMAN SOCIALITY

The rich history of ethical thought contains a wide range of views on issues too different to be presented accurately along a single continuum. These vary sharply both in their conception and in the considerations that are taken as basic. The most common comparison is one drawn between utilitarianism, or the ethics of prudence, and Kantian ethics, or the morality of conscience. These are not, as is sometimes thought, true opposites, since they do not differ on the same point but diverge sharply in approach. Utilitarianism is an ethic of action, endorsing the careful consideration of means and consequences with the purpose of obtaining maximum satisfaction. And since satisfaction is always a matter of personal experience, the seat of value and the touchstone for judgment lie wholly in the individual. The Kantian ethic, in contrast, focuses on motive, on intent, and the moral process is carried out through introspective examination and the decision of an autonomous will. Although all this is well known, it is important to recognize that both utilitarian and Kantian ethics are essentially theories whose moral center lies in the individual: it is the individual whose satisfaction or will determines the moral character of a situation. And although both theories take social considerations into account—the one by calculating the extent of satisfaction and suffering, and the other by the imperative of universalization—these extensions to a wider venue are secondary additions to what is at heart a private ethic.

Both the ethics of prudence and the morality of conscience rest on assumptions that are, in fact, articles of faith. Utilitarianism posits the ultimacy of the individual, a distinct and separate being located in a rational universe, whose intelligence is largely calculative. Mill's introduction of qualitative experience is a futile attempt to correct the private nature of quantitative judgments of pleasure, futile because it attempts to reconcile two antithetical factors: the personal character of experience and cultural standards of value. These factors are incompatible in practice as well as in theory, as social conflict and political controversy in our own day show only too well.

Kantian ethics has its own share of presuppositions, for it inherits the unhappy baggage of the dualistic tradition, locating the will in a hidden noumenal realm and denying the possibility of knowledge there "in order to make room for faith," as Kant bravely affirmed. Although Kant thought that he was providing an adequate grounding for morality, he mistook the uneasiness of his dogmatic slumber for an awakening, as Dewey once wryly observed. Seen in the way I have just described, both the morality of conscience and

the ethics of prudence are dogmatic philosophies: they make unto-
ward assumptions about experience, about knowledge, and about
values, assumptions that we now recognize to be fraught with difficulty and infused with error.

The last century and a half has seen important developments
in ethical and social thought that have moved beyond the dogmas
that burden the classic accounts. Attempting to overcome those difficulties, many of the later proposals appear to have taken sharply
different directions, although ironically the earlier assumptions
often reappear in new guises. In Nietzsche's case, the refreshing
transvaluation of values onto a naturalistic plane preserved elements of the individualism of Kant. Although pragmatism expanded utilitarianism's range of consequences and recognized the
inseparability of ends from the means of reaching them, it has had
difficulty finding a place for modes of rationality that are noncal-
culative and for modes of thought that are nonrational. Existen-
tialism recognized the pervasiveness of the irrational, yet even in
existential freedom one may find a radical Kantianism, with its
puzzling juxtaposition of subjectivism and universality. Although
it is unfair to pass over such significant contributions with a mere
gesture, we must content ourselves here with recognizing that they
have not succeeded in providing a satisfactory grounding for social
ethics. Many people, desperate for direction, have translated morality into technologies of thought control and behavior or have
moved on a contradictory course to seize on elements of self-tran-
scendence and mysticism in Eastern religion.[1]

Is it possible to restructure moral thought in a way that not
only avoids the dogmatic pitfalls of traditional ethics but also provides a theory less constrained by self-serving assumptions? Let us
explore some fresh directions to see whether we can discover a different approach to the problems of political philosophy. This will
require that we not just reconsider the assumptions of traditional
ethics but also ground ethics in a better understanding of human
thought, society, and culture.

Foremost in this rethinking of ethics is the recognition of the
essential sociality of human life. Philosophy lags far behind what
the human sciences have established here; for in both direct and

subtle ways, ethical theory continues to struggle with problems involving egoism, conscience, self, moral autonomy, and responsibility, problems structured in forms that preserve in one way or another the discreteness, the separateness of the moral individual. Reconstructing ethical thought on an understanding of humans as thoroughly social forces us to rethink these difficulties in radical ways—ways that follow the long-established tradition in philosophy not of solving such "problems" but of recasting them or even rejecting them entirely.

Consider some of the issues centering around moral responsibility. The traditional construction of the moral universe is one in which motives, decisions, and obligations rest in the autonomous individual: the self must freely make its own decisions and be judged by them, based on either its intent or its actions. What happens to this ordering of the moral situation if we discard the notion of the self-sufficient individual and recognize that this very self is a social construct and a social product? We cannot, then, speak of a single person, since persons do not come singly. Conflicts between egoism and altruism, self and other, are transformed into alternative social complexes in which personal and social factors are variously intermingled. The very notion of a moral universal, itself the outcome of an individualistic ethic as the sum of all individuals, must be transformed into degrees of generality that rest on social groups, not quantitative collections of separate selves. What this means is that morality is no individual matter but always a social one, that no values exist in isolation, and that moral issues arise in social situations and their resolution is a social process.

Ethical egoism and its contrary, altruism, are difficult to overcome. An eloquent illustration of their persistence is the feminist alternative to the theory of rights, the ethic of care. Care appears to be a welcome corrective to the self-preservative notion of rights. Indeed, it replaces the litigious focus of rights with generous motives of concern for others and with benevolent actions. Instead of calculating personal benefit, it directs our regard toward others. Care not only is in sharp contrast to narrow self-interest but also makes a noble addition to a moral tradition of generosity and selfless service. Another form of altruism, care stands in contrast to the masculinist ethic of self-aggrandizement. At the same time, however, the ethic of care remains within an individualistic frame. It centers on particular cases, informs personal decisions, and motivates private acts.

There are alternatives to this egoistic frame. In discussing the inescapability of self-reference that takes the form of personal satisfaction in any presumably benevolent act, Dewey draws a critical distinction between acting *as* a self and acting *for* a self.[2] Although ethical egoism conflates these two actions, they are really quite different. Whatever action we perform, we cannot help acting in some sense *as* a self, since that is the condition of any deliberate action. In every action, a self acts, for there can be no action without someone performing it. This is quite different from performing an action directed to one's personal benefit, that is, acting *for* oneself. The fallacy in ethical egoism lies in regarding all cases in which one acts as a self as instances of acting for oneself, whereas the latter is only a special case of the former. Ethical egoism is, therefore, not a necessary universal condition but a contingent, particular one.

Another example of a nonegocentric ethic is Erich Fromm's distinction among selfishness, self-love, and self-interest.[3] From a psychotherapeutic perspective, these are quite different, Fromm claims. Selfishness is a form of self-aggrandizement, feeding one's weakness in a futile effort to overcome what is actually a kind of self-hatred. The effort is futile because no quantity of personal gain can fill a lack that is of an entirely different sort, a lack of genuine self-regard. Self-love, in contrast, is the precondition to loving others, not its opposition. It reaches out from strength, not weakness, and draws people together toward a common fulfillment. One's true self-interest does not lie in private satisfactions but in the ability to conjoin one's personal value with that of others, so that instead of our interests being opposed, we recognize them as interdependent.

What these two instances illustrate is how resolving the problem of ethical egoism does not require endorsing one side or the other of the egoism-altruism alternative. It lies instead in surpassing both, that is, in restructuring the ethical problem in such a way as to transcend the conflict. We begin to realize that self and other are not moral alternatives, because there is no separate self and no distinct other. Each is mutually implicated to such a degree that they cannot be thought of apart. Self is truly other, other truly self.

Ethics, therefore, is social ethics, morality is social morality, and any attempt to base ethics on the distinct and separate individual must fail because it rests on a fiction, even though it is a conventional and time-honored fiction. But rejecting an ethic centered on the self does not mean endorsing the disappearance of the person into an anonymous society and relinquishing all self-direction and responsibility. The dialectical opposition of individual and society is a product of the very ethical individualism I am questioning. In its place we discover the social human, a new concept for moral philosophy but an old reality of moral life.

Three different directions are possible: one that centers on the individual, another that centers on the group, and a third that joins them, not in the form of a synthesis, which is a consequent stage, but as a prior, first condition of being human—the social human. With some of the issues and ideas now before us, let us see how they are reflected in different conceptions of community. The characterizations that follow may not always appear in clear outline in ethical discourse, but they represent the dominant tone in many of the social forms we are part of, forms rarely chosen deliberately and often not clearly grasped.

THE RATIONAL COMMUNITY

The rational community is a community of individuals that sees society as an artificial construct and the state, as Hobbes characterized it, as a leviathan, a monster to be feared, opposed, and tolerated as an unwelcome necessity at best. The philosophy of this kind of community is generally utilitarianism, in one form or another, from Bentham's classic mode to Rawls's more recent adaptation. Central in the rational community is the individual, motivated by self-interest, guided by reason, and protected by rights. It is the model assumed by political liberalism and economic individualism. Habermas's defense of rationality belongs here, too, for even though he holds that the ego is formed in social relations, the social order consists for him in the relations of subjective selves with other such selves. Thus in the theory of the rational community, the essential antinomy of self and other underlies social experience, and the two remain irreconcilable.

What guides individual action in the rational community are prudential motives, a careful calculation of costs and benefits in which nothing is done spontaneously or gratuitously. When collaborative action occurs, it is only because people identify interests they hold in common. Common interest, in fact, is the vehicle of social action, whether in government, in law, or in the many interest groups that form and dissolve as the occasion demands. Acts of spontaneous generosity may occur in the rational community when people are moved by tragedy, great personal need, enthusiasm, or a powerful common threat, as in war. These, however, are exceptions to the rule and are always accompanied by opportunists on the prowl for ways to turn every circumstance to personal gain. Yet increasingly complex economic dependencies and increasingly sophisticated technologies require collaborative action and drive people together. So although the rational community continues to characterize the modern industrial nation-state, it is beginning to justify internationalism, whether in the form of free-trade zones, international corporations, or political union. All these, however, have been devised to secure personal, private benefits.

The rational community is more a form of social order than a community, for whatever is common is so merely by the circumstantial concurrence of private interests. The principle of individualism infiltrates every deliberate action and each social domain. Economically, the rational community justifies a pattern of activity in which every individual pursues his or her self-interest. Because such interests rest on need and desire, and desire is never satiated, and because an economy of scarcity never provides enough to satisfy everyone, competition is pervasive. Opposition characterizes all economic relations—those among the producers and suppliers of services, those among the purchasers of goods and services, and those between both groups. A society of individuals pursuing separate and opposed interests also means that political decisions are made with the view to satisfying special interests. Such interests are represented formally by the electoral mechanisms of political democracy, in which everyone expresses his or her interests by casting a single vote, but they are represented informally and more potently by lobbies, pressure groups, and powerful economic and political organizations that promote their own interests by campaign contributions and by soliciting and manipulating blocs of "individual" votes using ethnic, racial, religious, and monetary appeals and promises.

Although the rational model is best known in its political and economic expressions, it pervades the social order. The rational ideal informs social thought in the idea that we exist as persons separate and apart from society, in the belief in individual autonomy, and in the conviction that personal freedom is secured only through watchful opposition to government action. In an adversarial system of law, the rational model is central to the judicial process. With a belief in free will, which endows each person with moral autonomy, the rational model stands at the center of conventional morality. Even the goals of psychotherapy—emotional independence, wholeness, self-sufficiency, and freedom—reflect this individualistic social ideal. Moreover, the therapeutic process's fixation on the "self"—on self-development and the cultivation of self-confidence and assertiveness—reflects the same individualistic bent. Such a psychology encourages self-absorption and rationalizes aggressiveness, its characteristic and common behavioral form. Finally, a whole philosophical industry is at work supporting the status quo of the rational society. Going well beyond utilitarian philosophy, the preeminent concept of the ego appears in the various forms of subjectivism and intersubjectivity, and in the correlative "problem" of the other.

Any alternative to this interplay of interests is difficult to envision, so deeply has the ideology of the rational society become rooted in the modern mentality. Yet signs of change have begun to appear with increasing frequency—signs of forces undercutting the premises of the rational community.

First among these changes is the growing recognition that self-sufficiency, one of the dominant cultural myths of Western societies, is a false ideal. It has always been an exaggeration, since wherever the ideal of self-sufficiency has been pursued, it has rested on a social bedrock. Embracing the model of economic independence, the pioneer or homesteader not only brought along equipment and supplies but also used a vast body of knowledge and technology developed and accumulated by thousands of generations of hardship and trial. The case is no different with more modern self-made persons. This exposes the fallacy in economic self-interest: that interests are fundamentally private and opposed, and that the independent, conflicting pursuit of those interests, which we call competition, is the best mechanism to their greatest fulfillment. Even that arch individualist Hobbes recognized that benefits beyond mere survival require social order and collaborative action, and Adam Smith himself recognized that sympathy binds a person to the feelings and motives of others. Individualism, it turns out, rests on a social foundation.

Yet doesn't acknowledging the necessity of social connections and cooperation represent a retreat from the rational model of the autonomous, self-sufficient individual, a noble ideal that has guided so much of the recent history of Western civilization? Isn't the social human merely a way of accepting inadequacy and dependency? This expression of the difference between the individual and the social is tendentious, however, for it assumes the viewpoint of individualism in order to impute inadequacy to the concept of human sociality. From its own standpoint, the idea of the social human is an affirmation. Instead of dependence, it affirms the ideal of an interrelatedness that is a form of mutual support, an increase in strength and well-being rather than an admission of weakness. And perhaps, in the final analysis, the self is more a folk category than it is an entity.

It is useful at this point to look more closely at the difference between dependence and mutuality. In a world of self-contained individuals, dependence is pervasive. In its sexual form, it is found both in taking the other and in giving oneself up to the other. In marriage, it is monogamy imposed from without through legal forms and social pressure. In social groups, it appears as hierarchical organization and as the suppression of minorities and the weak. It takes political form in the quest for power over others and in the cult of the leader. Psychologically, dependence appears equally in selfish behavior and in selflessness, as Fromm pointed out, the one intended to strengthen a separate self, the other to evade personhood. All these express the weakness of dependence, because they derive their force from a source that lies beyond the person. Far from promoting self-sufficiency, rational individualism actually fosters dependence. Nor does dependence provide greater strength; it actually reinforces the weakness it claims to ameliorate by focusing energies elsewhere and leaving the person still exposed.

Mutuality, in contrast, is not a sign of emotional or psychological insufficiency. Rather, it recognizes the fundamental incompleteness of the individual. Seen in this way, mutuality is not an admission of weakness or a defect. Instead, it acknowledges that we achieve fulfillment through harmonious connections with others, with social forms, and with environment, connections that implicate and change the things involved. Mutual supportiveness also takes many forms. Biologically, it consists in promoting life through the family and other kinds of domestic arrangements. Psychologically, it recognizes the manifold ways in which we develop character and personhood through relations with others. Mutuality finds the conditions for personal growth in voluntary forms of social relation, where each person is inseparable from the other. Even environment must be reconceptualized, changing from surroundings regarded as separate from ourselves to a matrix that is continuous with and includes us, a constant process of reciprocity among all the factors that constitute it.[4] Among nations, too, an awareness of mutuality is slowly increasing, not through alliances and the various forms of political domination, all of which express dependency, but in new legal relations and forums, such as the United Nations, the European Union, and the World Court, and in the gradual realization that national sovereignty is a political myth that has lost its usefulness. Economically, too, mutuality appears in the recognition of how common interests can be served by carefully expanding trade relations, removing barriers, and replacing economic exploitation with forms of assistance that benefit both the donor and the receiver. Mutuality even assumes a global scale as we recognize that pollution does not observe national boundaries, nor do many natural resources, and that industrial practices and commercial policies and products frequently have planetary consequences. All these expressions of mutual support rest on the premise—a fact rather than an assumption—that our fulfillment as persons and as societies is part of a single process and a single condition involving multiple factors. "Person," indeed, becomes a social category, the node of intersecting connections.

THE MORAL COMMUNITY

A second basic social form is the moral community. Unlike the community of self-interested individuals, the moral community rests on the insight that multiple bonds connect people with one another. It recognizes that people are interdependent and the relationships among them reciprocal. The ethical foundation of the moral community is the morality of conscience, and its classic formulation can be found in the philosophy of Kant. For him, moral obligation is the binding force that holds beyond desire or usefulness. An inner self ultimately stands alone with its moral choice. We may not desire the demands of morality and we may choose to disregard them, but this has no effect on their moral authority. The will must determine its own guiding principle, yet in doing this it represents every rational being. In this way, the morality of the individual becomes the force that unites humankind.

This version of the moral community shares two essential features with the community I just discussed—its rationality and its ultimate individualism. Qualifying the individualism of the moral community, however, are internal forces that press toward a larger order, embracing and joining morally separate beings into an uneasy confederation of the private and the social. For Kant, this is the powerful stipulation of universalization, which frames the moral demand so that it can extend to everyone. In authoritarian societies, the ethic of hierarchy binds individuals into a pyramid of power. As this amalgam becomes more complete, it may reach a point at which the members not only identify with the community but become utterly absorbed by it, relinquishing independent judgment and personal decision. When the moral community so overwhelms and suppresses individual volition, it has turned into something different, an organic community.

The organic community can assume a variety of forms. In a rigidly structured hierarchical order, power filters downward from its pinnacle, from level to increasingly broader level, each deriving a lesser degree of power from above until none remains at the bottom. In an autocratic society, a single leader exercises complete power while its members are subsumed in the whole, achieving their identity, their very being, as a part of that whole. Although institutional good is the binding element in the organic community and the ethos of the group glorifies social feeling, an authoritarian center of power and privilege wields the influence and dispenses the goods. To varying degrees and in distinctive ways, most religious groups, quasi-religious cults, military organizations, and corporations exemplify this kind of community. In its most extreme form, the organic community absorbs its members into the corporate body, withholding the ability to perform any independent action, any autonomy of will, and any vestige of identity apart from the group, all in the interest of devotion to some "higher" call. The organic community achieves its most complete development in the fascist state or fanatic movement, where the moral imperative of "blood and soil," ethnic purity, national destiny, or religious orthodoxy sucks up all separate wills into the irrepressible force of an exclusive community.

These modes of community—the rational, the moral, and its derivative, the organic—are limited, for the quality of human relations they engender lacks a genuine continuity of individual and social. Coolly calculating one's rational self-interest, standing bravely in moral isolation and futilely seeking society through intersubjectivity while lost in the endless depths of a searching conscience, absorbed into the anonymity of a faceless group— these forms do not succeed in developing the precondition for genuine community: a unity of individual and social in which neither dimension dominates but each enhances the possibilities of the other.

THE AESTHETIC COMMUNITY

Such a unity is what the aesthetic community aspires to. This third form of community moves beyond customary ways of thinking, so even though it resembles the other modes in some ways, we must avoid the temptation to assimilate it to them. The aesthetic community is not an order of individuals in either the rational sense or the moral one; nor is it a community whose participants relinquish their individuality and deliver themselves into the hands of a leader or become absorbed by a corporate identity. Its fundamental features are distinctive, so that to grasp the aesthetic community we must stand outside the convenient, conventional categories by which we usually order our understanding of human relations and social groups.

Every community proclaims some kind of unity, sometimes more in word than in fact. Organic unity, in which the parts have no separate existence but are bound to and subsumed under a whole, is often taken as the paradigmatic sense of unity. These parts may have a distinct identity, but they lack independence. Like the limbs and organs of a living creature, the underlying metaphor, the parts function within a whole from which they derive their meaning and value. Although organic unity is sometimes ascribed to a work of art, the aesthetic bond is actually quite different. Art carries a more subtle sense of connection that illuminates the aesthetic significance of community, a bond best described by the similar though not cognate word *continuity*.

Continuity is not absorption or assimilation, nor is it an external relation between separate things. It suggests, instead, connectedness within a whole rather than a link between discrete parts. Much as William James argued when he maintained that relations are not external connections but have an immediacy that is directly present and real to experience, relationships in a fulfilled community are not imposed from without but are inherent in the situation in ways that are concrete and functional.[5] The aesthetic community exemplifies this. Internal relations are, indeed, one expression of continuity. The connections among the members of an aesthetic community are as real, as much a part of the community, as the people themselves. Not only does this community possess no sharp boundaries; it has no deep divisions. Nor is there any sense in which the society or state is separate from the people who compose it. Their relation does not rest on internalized control (the moral model), on independence and self-sufficiency (the rational model), on isolation (both the moral and the rational models), or on domination (the organic model). Mutuality and reciprocity among the participants in an aesthetic community replace the barriers and separations that mark the other social modes.

Continuity allows for differences, although these are usually marked by a spectrum of gradations rather than abrupt changes. Sharp contrasts may occur, but these remain as part of a larger harmony. This sense of continuity is not vacuous. It denotes a merging that joins things already bound together rather than a combination of distinct and separate elements. As the different motivic and thematic components of a symphonic movement contribute to the character of the total auditory experience by their contrasts as much as their resemblances, human continuities denote a bond that overrides differences. Fusion takes place on a more basic level.

One sense of continuity is both perceptual and material: the understanding of our body as incorporating the food we ingest, the air we breathe, the clothes we wear, the objects we use, the place we inhabit, and the experiences we have. Consciousness is also part of this perceptual continuity, for whether we describe ourselves as embodied consciousnesses or reflective organisms, multidimensional continuities unite our cognitive, volitional, and physical dimensions. Human beings have continuity, too, with nature. Nature, as we live it, is environment—not external surroundings but the matrix of physical features and their order of meanings in which we are contributing, synergetic participants.[6] It is in these continuities that unify people and environment that community arises. Here are the connections of place, of human association, of language. Here too are the temporal connections of personal experience, tradition, and history. What makes such continuity aesthetic is the kind of unity it describes: a continuum of body, of consciousness, of context, all joined in the pervasive continuity of perceptual experience.

We can discover the aesthetic community, in a germinal sense, in the relationship between close companions or friends, where a bond may evolve that leads people to surpass the conventional limits of the self to attain what Aristotle called perfect friendship. By this he meant friendship between those who are good and who so desire the good of the other that each is able to feel the other's experience as in some way coincident with his or her own.[7] In a community of friends, the self expands to include the friend and cannot be known separately: the thought of the one is always inhabited by the presence of the other.

The erotic community may be more familiar. This community of lovers joins people in a multidimensional unity conventionally described as physical, emotional, and spiritual. What is important here is that the erotic community represents a connection that transcends the customary boundaries that isolate people. It is the closest many of us come to the sense of community I call aesthetic, not through a loss of self in sexual ecstasy but by the dissolution of protective barriers and a heightened awareness of self-with-other. This is an entirely different matter from purely sexual release, whose satisfaction is short-lived and easily narrows into the isolation of self-gratification. These germinal aesthetic communities of friendship and the erotic may not be residential or continuous in time; they are more likely to be circumstantial and may not endure.

Still other sorts of occasions offer an intimation of the aesthetic community. One is the bonding within the aura of the sacred that sometimes accompanies religious experience. In the feelings of sisterhood and brotherhood, of love and charity, and with ultimate generosity of spirit, the religious community dissolves the boundaries that separate people and approaches aesthetic continuity. However, the element of transcendence in the religious and its tendency toward the mystical distinguish it from the aesthetic, which centers instead on immediacy and presence. Another occasion of connectedness occurs in the intimacy of our appreciative experience of art, where a unity may develop that is the prototype of the aesthetic community. At its most generous and powerful, our engagement with art creates a continuity of experience that joins artist, appreciator, art object, and performer in a heterogeneous field of continuous forces. This is the qualitative source of the aesthetic community.

In the past, some philosophers recognized forms of bonding that anticipated the aesthetic mode of community. Locke claimed that society, with its relations and obligations, exists in a state of nature under the sway of natural law before any agreement to organize into a formal order. Nietzsche had the insight that the unifying aesthetic experience exemplified by Greek tragedy offers the ground for life in society, for communality. Husserl's idea that everything must be seen in context and within the horizon of the world in which it is presented led him to the notion that the life-world is made up of communities that exist in a social and historical setting.[8]

What, then, is an aesthetic community? What kind of phenomenon does the term describe, or is it merely an assumption, an ideal, a construct, a fiction? Does the aesthetic community realize continuity through certain kinds and networks of relationships? Like all language that does not denote a preformed object, the concept is an approximation, an attempt to locate and identify something that has the force of significant reality but has not yet been formulated.

The difference between an observer's and a participant's perception of a social situation may help us gain a clearer grasp of the aesthetic community. What an observer sees as clearly demarcated and structured may be fluid and responsive to the participant. Because both the rational community and the moral community are at bottom communities of individuals, they often ironically reflect the contrast between observer and participant. A person can think of himself or herself as an American individualist yet be enclosed in a stifling corporation or a charismatic movement, have an overbearing spouse yet feel comfortably married, be politically powerless yet be an ardent patriot. Conversely, one can be part of a close family or other intimate group yet feel alienated from it, insecure, lost, helpless, a stranger in a familiar land.

Forms of control are understood somewhat better now than in the past. We can see how this split between the world of the participant and that of the observer may be fostered by state-organized societies that are inimical to community and the strength it provides. People often experience realities falsely, and societies may deliberately foster false consciousness. From thought control and news management to outright censorship, the state, whatever its ideological persuasion, is adept at manipulating its members, managing from the standpoint of an observer its citizen participants. In all these cases, observer and participant occupy different orders; they speak foreign languages that are not easily translated and communicated.

The difference between observer and participant is preserved in the rational and the moral communities. Both the rational calculator and the inner conscience form their judgments and make their choices apart from the domain of action. In the aesthetic community, however, the contrast between observer and participant develops more subtly. These stances do not occupy different realities, each of which may be false to the other, as in the other modes of community. They rest instead on the same level, and when the awareness of an experience becomes but a different dimension of that very experience, they inform one another. Because the participant is, as such, actively engaged in community, this engagement becomes the primary mode, and the self-awareness of observation is secondary and dependent. The observer who is not a participant cannot truly grasp an aesthetic community. Both observer and participant must inhabit the same harmonious realm.

The aesthetic community is a community in and of experience. Its resemblance to the situation in which we experience art lends it its name. In art, when the potential of the aesthetic field is fulfilled, a rich reciprocity develops among the artist's creative force, the art object, its appreciator, and the performer or activator of the work. Contemplative distancing and the objectifying attitude adopted by the cognitive process are foreign to this situation. Instead, aesthetic engagement defines its character. The same reciprocity of constituent elements, the multiplicity of interrelated functions, the assimilation of observer into participant, the salience of qualitative experience—all these distinguish the aesthetic community as well.[9]

In a compelling passage in *I and Thou*, Martin Buber describes the personal encounter that establishes what he calls the world of relation.[10] Unlike ordinary experience, in which we objectify and manipulate things, a person in the intimacy of relation develops a personal bond with what is ordinarily considered quite distinct and separate. The kinds of things with which we can engage in this way, Buber shows, are perhaps surprising: first nature, then people, and ultimately art.

Nature we regard as the exemplary object of the sciences. Its philosophical ramifications excite the foundational questions of metaphysics and particularly of ontology—questions of order, of purpose, and ultimately of the very meaning and being of reality. Yet the usual way of understanding nature, both for science and for philosophy, rests on objectification and analysis. The same attitude is directed toward understanding human beings. Over the past century and a half, the social and behavioral sciences have taken the field in their examination of human orders and institutions. Until recently, their cognitive process tended to follow the same scientific and philosophical model of disinterested objectivity and rational analysis.

Yet our relation both with nature and with people can transcend the objectification with which we ordinarily distance them. In what Buber calls "life with nature," we join in a relation of undivided reciprocity with things in nature. In "life with men" we do not separate ourselves from others but experience a personal connection that unites us. But it is in the third of Buber's orders, "life with spiritual beings," that the transformative process of intimacy reveals itself most compellingly. It may seem strange for Buber to place art here, but once we recognize in it the act of origination, of discovery that has not found its tongue before, we realize how fully art epitomizes this highest life.

Life with spiritual beings does not appear just in the objects and occasions we fashion by our art. It pervades the kind of *experience* we associate with art objects and by which we identify them as such—aesthetic experience. Such experience, however, is not the exclusive province of art; it can be extended to embrace nature as well. More to the point here, this experience also encompasses the human. In the world of relation, we do not objectify, rationalize, order, and control people or things but rather enter into an intimate association with them. Buber's relation describes a bond that does not merely combine discrete entities but involves an open generosity with which we establish a deep, internal connection.

Further, in the world of relation we find more than a connection; we find a continuity. And eventually we discover even more: a community or, more specifically, what I have been calling an aesthetic community. A social aesthetic joins an aesthetic of art and an aesthetic of nature into an aesthetic of humans. All three of Buber's modes of relation—with nature, with humans, and with art—are domains of the same aesthetic realm, a remarkable coalescence of diverse orders into a single, embracing unity of experience. What science has divided into the natural world, the human world, and the mythological world; what philosophy has separated into metaphysics, ethics, and the philosophy of art—all regain their primal unity in the experience of the aesthetic.

Understanding Buber's world of relation helps us envision the aesthetic community. Here a social aesthetic joins humans and environment in multidimensional reciprocity. As the human environment consists not of places and buildings alone but of their complex interconnections with human participants and uses, an aesthetic community recognizes the social dimension of environment and the aesthetic conditions of human fulfillment.[11]

These forms of community—the rational; the moral, with its offspring, the organic; and the aesthetic—are clear forms. They are ideal forms of a sort but not unattainable "ideals," for they occur in different spheres and in a variety of ways. By identifying instances of these communities and by articulating their character and differences, we can know better how to live in them and how to guide and perhaps alter them. More important still, grasping the significant alternatives in community also enables us to make a deliberate choice about which to pursue. Thus what stands here as a study in political theory and social philosophy becomes, at the same time, a matter of political science and practice, and perhaps also the cardinal occasion of applied aesthetics. It suggests a qualitatively different direction for social inquiry and the need for a different kind of understanding. At this stage in social evolution and at this millennial point in human history, is any understanding more compelling than an aesthetic one?

Chapter Ten

Reflections on a Reflection: Some Observations on Environmental Creativity

The wild geese fly across the long sky above.
Their image is reflected upon the chilly water below.
The geese do not mean to cast their image on the water;
Nor does the water mean to hold the image of the geese.
—*Chinese, eighth century*

One commentator on this poem discovers a metaphor for creativity in the idea of reflection. Even though the geese have no thought of their image on the water or the water below any intention of reflecting their flight, it is at the moment of that reflection that their beauty appears most purely.[1] Where is beauty born, then? And how can creativity lie in reflection?

Reflection is a pregnant metaphor yet a troublesome one. The geese do not see their image, and the water is hardly aware of what appears on its surface. In fact, neither geese nor water nor image actually exists; there is nothing but a poem about them. The only artist is the poet, yet the commentator attributes beauty not to the poem but to the reflection. Like that evanescent image on the surface of the water, the beauty of the geese, wherever it is, seems to depend on something more.

* * * * *

To discover creativity here, moreover, is curious, even puzzling. We associate creativity most commonly with art and an artist, yet where in the scene is the art, where is the artist? Where, indeed, is the precondition of both—the capacity of aesthetic perception, a deliberate and focused engagement of appreciator and object? Nature is not art or artist or appreciator. Taking nature in its pristine unself-consciousness, we are at a loss to find even beauty here unless we are Platonists, for whom the world and its qualities are a pale image of the eternal verities, a reflection quite different from that of the wild geese on the chilly water. How, in fact, can creativity occur in the natural environment?

The most immediate idea of this environment is nature in its unaltered state, unsullied by human intervention. Sometimes fragile and fleeting in the snow-covered landscape or the sunset, sometimes sublime, as in the looming mass of a mountain, the thundering rush of a waterfall, or the impenetrable thickness of a primeval wilderness, environment, we often think, is nature alone, pure nature. This seems an unlikely locus for creativity, a process we usually consider distinctively human, requiring in its most basic sense the capacity to originate something. Is environmental creativity, then, an oxymoron? An answer may lurk here, but perhaps, like the geese, we can arrive at our destination most directly by flying a great circular route.

What is involved in the idea of creativity? More basic even than the model of an artist is the sense of bringing something into existence. This meaning of creativity, although identified with the artist or even with a god, is actually broader still. Its Latin origin (*creatus*) means to bring something into being, to cause to exist, and its Indo-European root (*krē*) means to grow or cause to grow.[2] This allows the agency of creative activity a wide span. Although there is action in bringing something into existence or making it grow, there is nothing in this that requires a human or superhuman agent. It is just as plausible to consider natural forces creative, not only in a figurative sense but also quite literally, since through their agency things are constantly brought into existence. At times, certain natural objects may actually resemble the work of an artist, as in the contorted shapes, rough surfaces, hollows, and holes of the limestone rocks pulled up from the bottom of Lake Tai in China. These objects can evoke an aesthetic response as profound as great sculpture, and they are sometimes mounted on pedestals and displayed as such. So extraordinary is the "artistry" of these natural forms that in gardens across China there are artificial rocks imitating them, and though they are the product of human action, they often have the lifelessness of a poor copy.

The idea of creativity must be refined still further, for actions of the most mechanical and unimaginative sort can produce things that were not there before. Is some kind of intelligence required for the process to be creative, an intelligence not governed by formulas or mechanical calculations of the means necessary to achieve a precisely defined, predetermined end? One can think of art created by intelligent people that one would never call creative, in any honorific sense. And all the mechanical, bland, routine kinds of making that require a certain intelligence in our automated world hardly qualify as candidates for aesthetic value. Moreover, even if creative intelligence is of a different sort, any manner of intelligence presumes rational thought of the kind humans are said to possess. The only intelligence we can ascribe to nature, then, is what we project onto it in self-congratulatory fashion.

Creativity must be more, then, than bringing something into existence, more than action directed intelligently. Perhaps we should add an element of openness, for creativity is not a calculated act but one that is open to the unexpected, an act that bears the touch of serendipity. It seems to be the antithesis of carefully planned action governed by an end determined in advance. When creativity is channeled between straight concrete banks, its living force is constrained to follow a docile and predictable course and soon vanishes. Although artists often proceed according to a general plan, this usually changes constantly along the way. Its fulfillment is never a separate stage but comes only as the completion of the creative process.

Creativity is sometimes thought to lie in originality; however, this is both too restrictive and insufficient. There are degrees of originality. If creativity connotes a high degree of aesthetic value, it sometimes happens that some of the most original artists do not produce the highest art. They may achieve influence, or even notoriety, but not always greatness. Erik Satie may have been unusually innovative and Bach remarkably content with the Baroque style and forms handed down to him, yet the one is surpassed by many and the other by none. Duchamp's art startles us by its meanings, but Braque's power lies in his painting.

Aesthetic creativity, then, requires more than originality. Unlike idealists such as Croce, who found art to lie in vision or intuition, most writers agree that art must also have its embodiment in a skillfully fashioned object of some sort, a working out, the *work* of art.[3] Creativity is not exclusively an inner state or an internal activity; it is *intentional*, always in relation to something. This need not be a physical object, like a statue or a building. The dancer has her dance, the poet her poem. Even the performance artist shapes an event. In all cases, something exercises a separate role in the aesthetic field—recalcitrant material or an imaginative object that makes demands on the artist as it does later in its finished form on the audience. Creativity occurs, then, in a context, as a field event in relation to some kind of object, which relies on the forces that produced it. This brings us back to environment, for we may say that creativity, as contextual, is always in a sense environmental.

ENVIRONMENTAL CREATIVITY

Our grasp of environmental creativity, however, is still not complete. The idea of environment, as I characterized it earlier, may have seemed clearer at first than creativity. Yet it is probably more dangerous to take our intuitions of concepts at face value than it is to accept our initial sense of people, and the consequences are likely to be more general. The meaning of environment is especially deceptive, for the very ease with which we seem to grasp the notion masks its essential complexity.[4] It may be worth reminding ourselves of how we have come to understand the idea as this book has proceeded.

We typically regard environment as surroundings, and there are good etymological reasons for this. Yet here is a case in which an entire cultural tradition requires reconsideration, not merely as an exercise in intellectual imagination but as a consequence of the serious environmental problems that confront this planet. Implicit in the idea of surroundings is the belief that there is an essential difference between us and our environment, and this belief creates a divisive sense of distance. This belief actually misrepresents the relation, for instead of being separated, we are bound to our environment by a network of interwoven and reciprocal influences. Indeed, these influences are not bonds at all but connecting lines that, like a circulatory system, carry on a continuous exchange between the human organism and its environment. This image may be too linear, for organism and environment are not separate but linked entities; they form a matrix of interacting forces that together assume their distinctive character.

Continuities, not separations, mark the human-environment complex, and these continuities are so fundamental that neither component can be thought of apart from the other. Environment embraces all the forces that constitute the human setting. It includes the built environment as well as natural features. And it is not only physical. The cultural matrix within which human life is embedded is an essential part of environment: the land-use patterns and the changes people have imposed on their landscape; the climate as it has been influenced by these changes; the language, institutions, belief systems, and forms of behavior of the groups who inhabit it; and most of all the inhabitants themselves. The list is a long one, but only by taking these factors together can we arrive at a full sense of environment. This collective range of influences enables us to recognize cultural landscapes, environments shaped by cultural influences and practices and unknowable apart from them. And it allows us to include the social environment, a dimension inseparable from these others. As humans, we live as part of what might be thought of as a natural-cultural ecosystem. In addition to the wholeness of the human-environmental field, we must include the fact that environment is dynamic. It is not just *in* process; it *is* process. Change is inherent in environment, and this gives it a temporal dimension, not just spatial ones.

Environment, then, is this inclusive, integrated, dynamic complex. To understand creativity, we must grasp it as part of the total environmental process. But before I proceed to consider this central issue, let me return to the arts, for they offer a model of how creativity grows.

Much can be said about creativity in the arts. I have already noted that creativity is not mechanical, it is not dominated by a goal to which everything is subordinated, it is not exclusively a matter of originality, and it does not require a human maker. Complementing these negativities is the essential complexity of the creative situation, in particular the fact that it is intentional. Creativity, as we have seen, is more than a purely internal, psychological process. It is directed toward a subject matter, a material that is to be fashioned, be it physical, imaginative, or perceptual. This last point is particularly important, because perception is central in all environmental situations, as it is in art. And creation, entailing engagement with some kind of object, is, in the final analysis, a process of shaping the course of perception. Perception, then, invoking an intentional relation, is contextual. Like creativity, it is a field event.

Here lies our clue, for if creation brings something into being through a process of fashioning perceptual materials, it need not be taken exclusively as the artist's prerogative, as an arcane activity that transpires only in the recesses of the studio. Whoever or whatever participates in such a perceptual process creates something. Creative activity occurs, therefore, not only in the artist's productive activity but also in the appreciator, who, through a reproductive process, generates a perceptual order similar to the one the artist originated. And it can occur as readily *en plein air* as in a museum, within any environmental situation.

We find ourselves, then, back with environment, with the added recognition that appreciative re-creation is no different from the process of artistic creation. The concert hall or art museum is as much an environment as a meadow or a river, and the creative activity in the one is no different in its structure and process from creative engagement in the other: in both, people order their experience through active perception. We can readily see how a landscape architect or a master gardener has a creative role in shaping the natural environment. Yet the same kind of perceptual creation occurs when we position ourselves to enjoy a harmonious vista, respond to the invitation to follow a serpentine path, sail into the embrace of a secluded cove, or paddle a canoe gently through the sun-filled air along a curving shore.

Creativity, therefore, occurs when something new is brought into being. Both the artistic process and the natural process do this. That one is a conscious, intentional act that takes place in the studio and the other a causal complex that develops in a natural setting does not alter the fact of creation. We may be struck with aesthetic awe as much by the Grand Canyon or the sight of the towering Rockies as by the *St. Matthew Passion* or the Grünewald *Crucifixion*. We bring our perceptual engagement to all these occasions, and our contribution involves us in the process as creative or re-creative participants. The human perceiver, when an active participant, is a creative force in every environmental situation.

Yet environmental creativity in nature does not take place only in wild places. It can as easily be joined with an environment shaped by human uses. The agricultural landscape is a human creation, and so are the urban concretions and suburban spread that constitute so much of the built environment. Creativity need not be aesthetic in intent, either. A builder may be as oblivious as any natural process of the perceptual qualities of what he or she builds. One's interest may be exclusively in money, power, or status or simply in constructing a particular church or house to meet a specific need. Nor is creation necessarily beneficent or beautiful. People bring strip development and slums into being as surely as they build garden cities and parks. Creation is not always positive.

CREATIVITY AS PERCEPTUAL

Thus, creativity is a perceptual making, whether it be an original act or one that emulates it, physical construction or reflective ordering. And when our involvement with an environment is strongly perceptual, it takes on an aesthetic character. We then become participants in an aesthetic field in which we engage with the object of our attention, and this aesthetic engagement is a model of creativity.[5] Our focus may be environmental or it may be on an art object, and a particular lake, gorge, or waterfall has the same uniqueness we ascribe to a work of art. The aesthetic eye, like the lover's, finds wonder everywhere.

Two sorts of creative environmental engagement have now become clear. One is overt, those situations in which we act physically on environment to alter the landscape. The other is more restrained, when we participate with environment through active perception rather than physical action. This last often occurs by a kind of abstraction, actually an act of subtraction, in which we deliberately remove a disturbing or irrelevant element from our perceptual field. Just as the eye searches out its object and ignores distracting features that the camera would unthinkingly record, we commonly disregard dirty train windows to view the passing landscape, filter out the intrusive signs in a park, ignore the telephone poles that blight our urban streets and deface the countryside. We may not be aware of a low level of disfigurement, such as static during a radio broadcast, scratches on a phonograph record, or tape hiss. Other environmental features may be harder to ignore, such as commercials that disrupt a radio or television program, canned music in a doctor's office, or stereos blaring on a beach. Memory may utilize a more subtle form of perceptual abstraction, removing from recollection those elements that intruded on environmental experience, such as the noisy, jostling crowds in Yosemite National Park or the bitter wind on top of Mount Washington.

Aesthetic appreciation, then, is a creative act, one that takes developed skill and thoughtful determination, very much the same abilities that the artist employs in her work. It is a skill that we may bring to both our environmental experiences and the arts. Furthermore, we can expand some of the same aesthetic concepts we apply to art by assigning them to environment. Instead of identifying beauty with the formal perfection of an art object, it becomes the pervasive aesthetic value of an environmental situation. And we can measure that beauty not by its formal features alone but by the perceptual immediacy and intensity that enrich the intimate bond of person and place. Conversely, the scale has a negative side when such awareness is demeaning and repugnant.

The sublime is a particularly important aesthetic category in environment. It designates experience whose aesthetic force comes from the sense of being part of a perceptual matrix of overwhelming magnitude and power. This, too, has a negative form, particularly in industrial-commercial cultures where narrowness of vision, joined with an exploitative mentality, has created negative environments of overpowering proportions and inescapable scope.[6]

Whatever the case, environment transforms our understanding of creation. It enlarges an idea so important for the theory of the arts into an awareness of natural and human processes, coupled with the formative contribution of an active, participating perceiver.

Where, then, lies the beauty of the passing reflection as the geese fly overhead? It appears, I suggest, in our creative contribution as we grasp the fleeting image on the surface of the water. Here, however, this perception is purely imaginative, a vision we have only as readers of the poem. Yet in the intense awareness with which we engage in the situation as reader and viewer, we join the geese and the water in an act of creation.[7] In grasping their interplay in the reflection, we generate their beauty. And in reflecting on the poem, we create an aesthetic environment.

Chapter Eleven

Sacred Environments

It may seem unusual to introduce the sacred into a discussion of aesthetics. The one presumably deals with ultimacies and the other with appearances, although a certain resemblance between religious and aesthetic experience has occasionally been remarked on. Perhaps it is more plausible to consider the sacred when exploring aesthetic values in environment, for every culture consecrates certain places, such as houses of worship, tombs, and, by extension, national monuments and memorial buildings. Even so, *sacred* seems an unlikely term to apply to environment, for an environment is less a place than a situation, less a location than a context. Convention, however, has no monopoly on meaning but rests only on general agreement about the significance of a term, when such agreement exists. And the authority of convention depends only on the extent of agreement, not truth. Given the approach to environment that this book has developed, it is not surprising to suggest that, convention notwithstanding, such notions require rethinking—environment no less than place, sacred no less than aesthetic.

To the extent that a philosophical inquiry can be empirical, let us begin by considering four cases, each representing a particular type of sacred environment. Together they provide the grounds for a more general understanding of the environmental experience and meaning of the sacred.

FOUR SACRED ENVIRONMENTS

The first of these sacred environments centers on an object, in this case Brancusi's *Endless Column*, a large outdoor sculpture in Tirgu Jiu, Rumania. Set in a circular grass plaza, the column is constructed of geometrical steel modules piled to a height of nearly a hundred feet. Brancusi had used the same relatively simple modular form for the pedestals of far smaller sculptures, but magnifying its size and duplicating its pattern in a high vertical sequence transformed the shape. The *Endless Column* is no slender shaft but a series of large units, each the height of a person and nearly as broad. The pedestal has become a sculpture in its own right, a great soaring column that emanates extraordinary force, charging the surrounding space and enveloping the onlooker.

This is true of every good sculpture, to be sure, but the power of the *Endless Column* is remarkable. As one looks upward from its base, the column is true to its name, appearing to dwindle into infinite space. On entering the sculpture's field of force, the viewer's position and movement seem to affect the work, causing it to bend and twist in ways that have a reciprocal physical impact on the body of the onlooker. As one moves toward the column, the sculpture seems to tilt away, its elongated mass leaning precipitously backward. As one backs off, the pitch of the column changes, its great bulk bending forward at an increasingly threatening angle. As the viewer walks around the sculpture, the column appears to twist and spiral upward, its geometrical facets alternately reflecting light or obscured in shadow. Not only does the sculpture's force generate the space around it and charge it with energy, but the work magnetizes the viewer into a powerful dynamic relation with it. A new order has been created that joins sculpture with the human body.

A different type of sacred environment occurs in an interior space, in this case the Rothko Chapel in Houston, Texas. Visiting the chapel takes on the character of a pilgrimage, since it is an unobtrusive structure hidden on the campus of the University of St. Thomas, some distance from the center of the city. When the chapel is finally located, one enters a forecourt, a small rectangular plaza dominated by the steel form of Barnett Newman's *Broken Obelisk* set in a reflecting pool. Poised inverted, tip to tip above a pyramidal base, the truncated obelisk extends a profound reception to the visitor. As the pool reflects the planes of the sculpture, its precarious balance seems to extend that moment of equipoise to eternity. Yet as one walks around the pool, both the object and its reflection change, creating a magical mobility that resembles the dynamic movement of the *Endless Column* and producing, as a result, a dialectic of permanence and change. Meditation thus begins even before one enters the chapel.

The small, low doorway into the chapel leads to a wide but shallow antechamber, at each end of which is a modest opening into the inner, main chamber. The chapel itself is an open octagonal space containing fourteen large, somber, almost monochromatic gray canvases, four wooden benches facing the largest walls, and three meditation cushions.[1] Natural light comes from a large center skylight and is diffused by a reflecting panel beneath. Some visitors are disappointed by the low-key, understated interior; others are overwhelmed. A mere description cannot convey the peculiar force of this environment. It does not possess the architectural grandeur of a cathedral or the religiosity of a church. The sacredness of the chapel lies in the experience rather than the place. A quiet energy emanates from Rothko's art in this setting, filling the chapel and suffusing the enclosed space with a force profound and powerful. Some visitors feel its strength to such an overwhelming degree that, on entering the chapel, they find themselves weeping uncontrollably. Such art possesses an ontological dimension, joining with person and place to create a world of the sacred.

Yet another kind of sacred environment encompasses an open space. Jefferson Rock, near Harpers Ferry, West Virginia, is a great boulder atop a lofty prominence overlooking the smooth outlines of the lower surrounding mountains. Far below lies the silver surface of the confluence of the Shenandoah and Potomac Rivers. The Rock offers a striking vantage point from which to view the landscape in all directions. Here Thomas Jefferson once stood in wonder, and many both before and after him have come to admire the same scene. This dramatic experience of space is unusual for the way in which the viewer's presence gives the great expanse coherence and a center. Wallace Stevens, an American metaphysical poet of the twentieth century, offered a metaphorical description of such a situation in the "Anecdote of the Jar":

I placed a jar in Tennessee,
And round it was, upon a hill.
It made the slovenly wilderness
Surround that hill.

The wilderness rose up to it,
And sprawled around, no longer wild.
The jar was round upon the ground
And tall and of a port in air.

It took dominion everywhere.
The jar was gray and bare.
It did not give of bird or bush,
Like nothing else in Tennessee.[2]

What makes the view from Jefferson Rock so extraordinary is not any sense of power that comes from dominating the scene, such as the feeling mountain climbers report on achieving a summit. It is rather the awareness of being at the heart of an immense space and the source of its coherence. One stands at the center of a world that radiates outward. Although at a great height, the viewer is not above and beyond the scene but part of an immense universe that he or she orders and is enfolded within. Instead of feeling pride at so powerful a position, the viewer is characteristically overtaken by a deep sense of humility. Perhaps this comes from being encompassed by such greatness, perhaps from recognizing how small and vulnerable one truly is. In this form of sacred environment, the human presence creates and orders space on a cosmic scale, while at the same time being dependent on and integrated in it, as, on the microcosmic level, a nucleus is in its cell.

The final kind of sacred environment does not involve a relation with a particular object or place but centers on an experience of a dynamic and integrative character. This form of sacredness is perhaps more modest than the others, and its occasions may be more familiar and common: strolling through a Japanese garden, paddling down a quiet stream, walking along an unfamiliar woodland trail rich in detail, perhaps even driving at a leisurely rate along a scenic country road in the first green of spring. An evocative landscape, rich with interest and detail, may be absorbing but is still incomplete; it requires our thoughts, associations, knowledge, and responses. If an active interpenetration of person and place develops, a fusion may emerge that depends on our personal contribution, on how we activate the environment by engaging with its features and bringing them into meaningful juxtaposition with our memories and associations. When this fusion occurs with focus and intensity, the experience may acquire the peculiar yet charmed humility we associate with the sacred. And because its quality lies in an extraordinary experience rather than an extraordinary place, this type of exerience leads us to find the sacred in many environmental situations. But what is it that makes them sacred?

WHAT MAKES AN ENVIRONMENT SACRED?

Although it is useful to identify these different types of sacred environments—and there are surely others—it is important to recognize that they refer not to kinds of places but rather to different settings of experience. They make it clear that these places, without a human presence, are neither sacred nor even environments, for an environment results from a joining of person and place. Nor is the experience of such an environment simply an internal occurrence. Rather, such places succeed because they encourage active physical and perceptual engagement. Is there anything common to these kinds of environments that leads us to find them sacred?

A characteristic that appears both in the experience of art and in sacred environments is the sense that the occasion has a distinct and special significance that makes it unique. One is centered, perceiving things with enhanced acuteness and concentration. This is sometimes described as a magical moment in which the world becomes intensely vivid. One experiences such a close personal relation to the place that one's thoughts, attention, body, and senses are intimately engaged. A powerful feeling of connectedness displaces the protective distance we usually impose between ourselves and the places we encounter, a distance not only physical but psychological. This distance is sometimes cultivated in art as the "psychical distance" that is thought necessary for appreciation, but in art as in environment, it sacrifices the direct bond of engagement in order to focus on an object. Moreover, it is a false exchange, since perceiver and object are not discrete and separate but mutually supportive. Particularly in environment, one has the sense of being taken up, of being immersed in the situation, engaged in a total, binding condition. And at its most intense, such a situation evokes an aura of reverence. The very air seems hushed and charged; the environment has become sacred. This condition has a curious corollary in the transformation that takes place in the self. The sense of being disparate and detached diminishes and even vanishes, and the participant becomes inseparable from the place and the occasion.

Although we can consider the sacred from the standpoint of the participant's experience, we can also approach it from the conditions of such experience. Many features characterize a sacred environment, especially the strong sense of value that pervades the situation. Sometimes the historical significance of a place may put one in a reflective, reverential mood, receptive to associations with earlier personages, inhabitants, or events whose aura still lingers. The features of the place, indeed its very ground, possess a sense of importance, a preciousness in themselves. We experience the space as charged, intense with its own energy, not static but active. Such a space possesses a magnetic attraction, drawing us into its power and encouraging us to reciprocate by rapt attention and perhaps by movement. The conditions of the sacred develop a continuity with those who participate in it and become absorbed and integrated into the space.

These ideas resemble the Native North American understanding of human life in nature considered earlier.[3] Many of these tribal societies express views that are fundamentally religious in character. We are too willing to dismiss as primitive animism the sense that all creatures, things, and places have spiritual characters. Yet as our environment deteriorates, responsible governments and individuals are beginning to question the narrow faith in the technological domination of nature. This has led many to reconsider the ancient view and to recognize the profound insight such an idea embodies. We have begun to rediscover the preciousness of land, water, and air as a result of the often irrecoverable harm done to our environment by small interests and short-term objectives. Because environment is socially created and almost always common to many inhabitants, any damage to it has social as well as physical effects. The Native American grasp of the sacredness of the land is not a case of primitive piety but a deep and inescapable insight.

IMPLICATIONS OF SACRED ENVIRONMENTS

Grasping the nature of sacred environments has some curious consequences. Such environments, such events, tell us something about what all environment is. Not a place but an occasion, it is the world we experience. This makes the difference between environment and place clearer. A place is a physical location that we can enter and occupy. It is there independently—impersonal and self-sufficient—and a person who approaches and penetrates it is distinct and separate. We can describe places in impersonal terms because they do not depend on a human presence, for any such presence is merely contingent and irrelevant. An environment is different. It is more than surroundings, as environments are usually construed, more even than a relation with surroundings. An environment is a continuity of person and place, a situation that is more than the sum of its parts but a distinct, complete, and integral whole. This is intimated in what is sometimes called a sense of place—that is, place that has the special, binding quality I am ascribing here to environment.

Recognizing their differences also helps us distinguish between a sacred environment and a sacred place. A sacred place is a location that is honored or institutionally valued, such as a cathedral, synagogue, temple, sacred grove, or memorial. Its value presumably rests in itself, quite independent of anyone who visits it. A sacred environment, in contrast, engages and binds us as participants with a force and intensity that result in the kind of powerful occasion described earlier. Sacred places are sacred by decree. They may or may not evoke the kind of intense engagement that would transform them into environments; and if they do not, they are only formal objects of ritualized veneration and indifferent feeling.

Understanding the character of a sacred environment has another far-reaching implication. Because a sacred environment exemplifies environment most intensely, it also tells us something about how environment can fail. We see this best by distinguishing the sacred from the profane. To profane is to desecrate something, in this case to desecrate an environment. It involves an action that removes the sacredness of an environment by destroying the binding unity of person and place. Examples are all too common: eliminating living neighborhoods to make way for freeways, razing historic structures that give character to a district in order to erect impersonal office towers, displacing grand homes on older streets with a line of dull commercial structures, flattening and paving the green spaces surrounding cities into prosaic malls, channeling urban streams underground or hiding them between concrete embankments.

The dictionary defines "to profane" as "serving to debase or defile what is holy."[4] Yet in some sense, is not all land holy land? "Atoning" for such profanation, to continue the theological metaphor, means becoming reconciled, literally making what has been profaned "at one." And in this case, that involves making a failed environment sacred again. Furthermore, human activity can not only desecrate a place but also destroy the very possibility of environmental engagement, the very possibility of sacredness. Yet as people can profane environment, so they can atone for such desecration by reviving the possibility of environmental unity. Capable of destroying environment, we can also re-create it.

Environments that are so powerful as to be sacred may seem unusual, far from ordinary experience. We are accustomed to observing the sacred on special occasions under prescribed conditions and carefully choreographed rituals. Although this may be customary, it is not necessary. In fact, because this practice isolates the sacred, it allows violence to be perpetrated on the rest of our world. If only special places and rare environments are sacred, then the balance of the human world becomes disvalued and a ready victim to desecration. But the Native North Americans had a different sense of things that can guide us here. For them, a power inheres in every object and place, be it stone, tree, lake, or sky. All must be treated with respect and reverence. A religious view of nature means that all nature is one's cathedral and worship is the usual attitude. The Jews' blessing before eating bread and the Christians' grace before meals are similar forms of reverential behavior that introduce the sacred into the mundane. Indeed, it does not demean the holy by sanctifying ordinary life but rather raises its value to the level of the sacred. No sharp division separates sacred from ordinary environments, for these are not opposites. There is rather a continuity between them, since value suffuses all environment. Any environment can become sacred, and any environment can be profaned. And all are capable of degrees.

I have mentioned the sublime in various places in this book, and at least as a positive characteristic of environment it seems to resemble the sacred. Both are experienced as possessing intense value. Both surpass the feeling of separateness and evoke an occasion that is overwhelming in its absorption. Both may involve natural occurrences of remarkable moment. Yet at least in its traditional signification, the sublime differs markedly from the sacred in other ways. The sublime is a feeling generated by contemplating an object or a scene—a thunderous waterfall or the starry heavens above—whereas the sacred is an experience evoked in a situation—from a religious ritual or a musical performance to a meditative stroll in a Chinese temple garden. Traditionally, the sublime also differs from the sacred in being essentially dualistic or at least by building on the contrast between an overpowering object and the perceiver's response to it. Historically and conceptually, the sublime rests on the opposition of subject and object. The sacred, in contrast, is a fusion, all the more overpowering in not being localized or centered.

But even when the sublime is freed from these traditional constraints and is conjoined with the perceiver, either positively or negatively, in aesthetic engagement, it remains different in character from the sacred. The sense of overpowering magnitude that identifies the sublime—power so immense as to render the human presence puny and insignificant—does not occur in the experience of the sacred. In the sacred there is neither intimidation nor fear but rather a sense of being expanded and uplifted, rendered precious through the radiance of the sacred. The fearsome thrill of the sublime is replaced by the warm suffusion of affirmation—perhaps joyful, perhaps tearful, but always positive. The sublime may be either positive or negative. The sacred is always positive, and the profane is its negation.

A parallel has sometimes been drawn between aesthetic and religious experience. Both are intensely absorbing, personal, and immediate. Both extend their directness and intimacy to bring one into a region of being that far exceeds the private domain attributed to subjectivity. This discussion of the sacred in environment is only tangentially related to religious experience and important differences remain between them; yet the aesthetic and the sacred share another characteristic: both have moral as well as aesthetic dimensions.

As in the experience of art, aesthetic value suffuses the sacred environment. Certainly both art and environment share our vivid perceptual interest. At the same time, the qualitative experience they generate has not only immediate value but also effects that extend beyond the perceptual present. Experiencing an environment as sacred may change our sense of the world and affect how we live and act. To regard the world as sacred and everything that is part of it as inherently valuable can change our decisions and alter our actions. It can also sensitize us to the profanation of the world and render unacceptable practices that we formerly ignored or acquiesced in unthinkingly. Recognizing and conserving environmental values, then, takes on ethical import and becomes a moral obligation. Moreover, there is a social interest in sacred environments—and, if all environments are potentially sacred, in every environment—just as there is a social interest in great art. As one can claim that the "owner" of such art has a moral obligation to preserve and share it, so one can hold that everyone who participates in an environment in any way has an interest in it and an obligation toward it. In environment, as in art, possession is never absolute; one is always answerable for one's treatment of it. Because moral and aesthetic values appear to some degree in all environments, both place an obligation on us individually and socially.

Sacred environments may develop, then, from the space generated by a radiant object, in an enclosed space charged with value, in open space made coherent through the human presence, through the dynamic interdependence of an active perceiver and an environmental order, and in still other forms. Moreover, since such environments are often not set apart from the ordinary course of experience, we can no longer regard them as rare and different. And because environments are sacred in varying degrees, our participating presence both contributes to their sacredness and influences its extent. Insofar as this confers a godlike power on humans, it confers on us an equally powerful obligation.

Although we may have begun by thinking of environment as a special, limited notion, these explorations have shown that it encompasses the entire human realm. In the process, the idea of environment has not lost meaning or clarity; rather, it has gained in resonance and value. Developing the idea has also expanded the reality, for we have ended by sacralizing the world and the human participation that is inseparable from it. The very grandeur of this conception of environment testifies to the value of its successes, the tragedy of its failures, and the endless richness of its possibilities.

Notes

CHAPTER ONE
Aesthetics and Environment

1. D. W. Meinig, ed., *The Interpretation of Ordinary Landscapes* (New York: Oxford University Press, 1979), 3.

2. The limited scope of traditional philosophical ideas of experience undermines the breadth and usefulness of the idea, and it fails to reflect the importance of the common experience of multisensory bodily engagement with the landscape.

3. Vincent Scully, *The Earth, the Temple and the Gods* (New Haven: Yale University Press, 1977), 186–215.

4. Christopher Tunnard, *A World with a View: An Inquiry into the Nature of Scenic Values* (New Haven: Yale University Press, 1978).

5. Chapters 3 and 4 develop this critical aesthetic process, the first in the extended example of Disney World, and the second by elaborating a critical apparatus for aesthetic judgment. A more general discussion of criticism appears in my book *The Aesthetic Field, a Phenomenology of Aesthetic Experience* (Springfield, IL: Charles C. Thomas, 1970). In *The Aesthetics of Environment* (Philadelphia: Temple University Press, 1992). chap. 9, I consider environmental criticism more specifically.

6. Aristotle, *Nicomachean Ethics* I.3.

7. David Hume, "Of the Standard of Taste," in *Essays* (1757); a classic text, frequently reprinted.

8. Chapter 4 discusses the negative judgment of landscape.

CHAPTER TWO
An Emerging Aesthetics of Environment

1. A Claude glass is a small viewer of convex black or colored glass, whose curved surface reflects the landscape in miniature and reduced color.

2. Ann Bermingham, "The Picturesque and Ready-to-Wear Femininity," in *The Politics of the Picturesque: Literature, Landscape and Aesthetics since 1770*, ed. Stephan Copley and Peter Garside (Cambrige: Cambridge University Press, 1994), 88.

3. This point is developed in Arnold Berleant, *Art and Engagement* (Philadelphia: Temple University Press, 1991).

4. Important recent literature in environmental aesthetics includes the following books and articles: Arnold Berleant, *The Aesthetics of Environment* (Philadelphia: Temple University Press, 1992); Arnold Berleant, "Architecture as Environmental Design," in *Art and Engagement* (Philadelphia: Temple University Press, 1991); Steven C. Bourassa, *The Aesthetics of Landscape* (London: Belhaven, 1991); Allen Carlson, "Appreciation and the Natural Environment," *Journal of Aesthetics and Art Criticism* 37 (1979): 267–75; Allen Carlson, "On the Possibility of Quantifying Scenic Beauty," *Landscape Planning* 4 (1977): 131–72; Allen Carlson, and Barry Sadler, eds., *Environmental Aesthetics: Essays in Interpretation* (Victoria, BC: University of Victoria, 1982); Salim Kemal and Ivan Gaskell, eds., *Landscape, Natural Beauty, and the Arts* (Cambridge: Cambridge University Press, 1993); Mara Miller, *The Garden as an Art* (Albany: State University of New York Press, 1993); Jack L. Nasar, ed., *Environmental Aesthetics: Theory, Research, and Applications* (Cambridge: Cambridge University Press, 1988); David Seamon, ed., *Dwelling, Seeing, and Designing: Toward a Phenomenological Ecology* (Albany: State University of New York Press, 1993); David Seamon and R. Mugerauer, eds., *Dwelling, Place and Environment: Towards a Phenomenology of Person and World* (New York: Columbia University Press, 1985); Yrjö Sepänmaa, *The Beauty of Environment* (Helsinki: Suomalainen Tiedeakatemia, 1986).

CHAPTER THREE
Deconstructing Disney World

1. As one frequent visitor remarked to me with evident conviction, "Disney World is the happiest place on earth." This turns out to be a line from Disney World publicity.

2. J. F. Lyotard, *The Postmodern Condition* (Minneapolis: University of Minnesota Press, 1984), 81.

3. The Disney Corporation alone owns 27 resorts and employs 39,000 people. By early 1992, Disney World had 17,000 guest rooms and 580,000 square feet of meeting space. Disneyland and Disney World

together are the top resort destinations in the world, and this is not an exclusively national phenomenon. Japan joined with the Disney Corporation to create Tokyo Disneyland, which opened in 1983 and had its 100 millionth guest in 1991; in 1992, EuroDisneyland opened just outside Paris.

4. In World Showcase, a crew dressed in legionnaires' garb (which for one visitor from the Third World had an uncomfortable association with colonialism) patrols the grounds removing the least scrap of paper. An Orlando paper once reported that workers shoot down vultures at night in an effort to remove a discordant element, a claim that Disney management roundly denied.

5. Besides its exhibits, Walt Disney World has established a college internship program that enrolls a thousand college students each year. These students spend an entire semester attending weekly classes at Walt Disney University, graduating with a "mouseter's degree" or a "ducktorite degree."

6. Donna Morganstern and Jeff Greenberg show how theme park visits can influence beliefs about the past in "The Influence of a *Multi-Theme Park* on Cultural Beliefs as a Function of Schema Salience: Promoting and Undermining the Myth of the Old West," *Journal of Applied Social Psychology* 18 (June 1988): 584–96.

7. Umberto Eco, "Travels in Hyperreality," in *Travels in Hyperreality* (New York: Harcourt Brace Jovanovich, 1986), 43; Stefan Morawski, "On the Subject of and in Post-Modernism," *British Journal of Aesthetics* 32, no. 1 (January 1992): 57.

8. Bob Shacochis, "In Deepest Gringolandia," *Harpers* 279, no. 1670 (July 1989): 42–50; Alun Howkens, "Peace of the Country," *New Statesman and Society* 2, no. 61 (August 4, 1989): 12–13; Alice Thomas Ellis, "Crumbling Urns," *Spectator* 261, no. 8350 (July 23, 1988): 34–35.

9. "Masterpieces of falsification" is Eco's phrase. "What it sells is, indeed, goods, but genuine merchandise, not reproductions. What is falsified is our will to buy, which we take as real, and in this sense Disneyland is really the quintessence of consumer ideology." Eco, "Travels in Hyperreality," 43.

10. Christopher Frayling has commented that the procession of facsimiles and simulacra in Disney–MGM Studies is about to supersede the real thing, so that "one day all of our streets will conform to the vision that Walt Disney saw." "Themes Like Old Times," *Punch* 298 (January 26, 1990): 30–33.

11. Magic Kingdom, for example, connects with children's fantasy

world outside the park. Kids can interact with characters such as Alice (in Wonderland), Mickey Mouse, Goofy, Pluto, Peter Pan, Cinderella, Dumbo, and Snow White. They recognize these characters from TV and act as if they know them.

12. Quoted in Eco, "Travels in Hyperreality," 43.

13. Lyotard, *The Postmodern Condition*, 81.

14. John Stuart Mill, *Utilitarianism* (Indianapolis, IN: Bobbs-Merrill, 1957), 14.

15. John Dewey, *The Quest for Certainty: A Study of the Relation of Knowledge and Action* (New York: Minton, Balch, 1929).

16. Maurice Merleau-Ponty, *The Visible and the Invisible* (Evanston, IL: Northwestern University Press, 1968), 91, 94.

CHAPTER FOUR
The Human Touch and the Beauty of Nature

1. John Ruskin, *The Elements of Drawing* (London: J.M. Dent, 1920), letter II. See also John Ruskin, *Nature Studies*, ed. Rose Porter (Boston: Dana Estes and Co., 1900), 112–13.

2. Pauline von Bonsdorff develops a somewhat different discussion of the meaning of nature in "Forest Aesthetics as Aesthetics of Forestry" (unpublished).

3. Thomas Gray, "Elegy Written in a Country Churchyard," st. 14. The entire stanza reads: "Full many a gem of purest ray serene,/The dark unfathom'd caves of ocean bear:/Full many a flower is born to blush unseen,/And waste its sweetness on the desert air."

4. Thomas Aquinas, *Summa Theologica* (c. 1270) Ia.q.39.a.8.

5. Ibid., I.q.2.a.3.

6. Courbet's painting, in the collection of the Musée d'Orsay, is also known as *Venus and Psyche*. *The Origin of the World* is in a private collection in Paris.

7. Gilbert Stuart's 1796 portrait of Washington is held jointly by the Museum of Fine Art in Boston and the National Portrait Gallery.

8. William Shakespeare, *Henry V*, act 5, scene 2. Kecksies are dried hemlock stems. I am grateful to Peter D. Paul for calling this passage to my attention.

9. The recent fashion of making new art that deliberately reworks well-known paintings from the canon clearly has nothing in common with forgery.

10. For the division of Chinese cities into walled wards, see Yi-Fu

Tuan, *Topophilia, a Study of Environmental Perception, Attitudes and Values* (Englewood Cliffs, NJ: Prentice-Hall, 1974), 176.

11. Aristotle suggested that the aesthetic and the moral are reciprocal when he noted that anything is beautiful "which, being desirable in itself, is at the same time worthy of praise, or which, being good, is pleasant because it is good." *Rhetoric* 1366a.

12. Chapter 3 uses the concept of the sublime in a similar way. Also see J. F. Lyotard, *The Postmodern Condition* (Minneapolis: University of Minnesota Press, 1984).

13. I discuss the relation between the aesthetics of art and the aesthetics of environment in *The Aesthetics of Environment* (Philadelphia: Temple University Press, 1992), chap. 6.

CHAPTER FIVE
Aesthetic Function

1. Jerome Stolnitz, "On the Origins of 'Aesthetic Disinterested-ness,'" *Journal of Aesthetics and Art Criticism* 20, no. 2 (winter 1961): 131–43. See also Arnold Berleant, "The Historicity of Aesthetics I," *British Journal of Aesthetics* 26, no. 2 (spring 1986): 101–11, and "The Historicity of Aesthetics II," *British Journal of Aesthetics* 26, no. 3 (summer 1986): 195–203.

2. Immanuel Kant, *Critique of Judgment* (1790), 5.

3. Arnold Berleant, *The Aesthetic Field, a Phenomenology of Aesthetic Experience* (Springfield, IL: Charles C. Thomas, 1970), chap. 3.

4. See Berleant, *The Aesthetic Field*, chap. 2.

5. Arnold Berleant, "Aesthetics and the Contemporary Arts," *Journal of Aesthetics and Art Criticism* 29, no. 1 (winter 1970): 155–68. See also M. Dufrenne, "The Aesthetic Object and the Technical Object," *Journal of Aesthetics and Art Criticism* 23, no. 1 (fall 1964): 113–22.

6. Kenneth Clark, *The Nude* (New York: Pantheon, 1956), 155–68; also 5, 20 ff.

7. See, for example, Walter Terry, *Ballet, a New Guide to the Liveliest Art* (New York: Dell Publishing, 1959), 11, 24; and John Martin, *Introduction to the Dance* (New York: Norton, 1939), 10.

8. Clark, *The Nude*, 8.

9. Martin, *Introduction to Dance*.

10. Such proximity, it is argued, impedes the attitude of detachment considered necessary for aesthetic appreciation. For a critique of this tradition, see Arnold Berleant, "The Sensuous and the Sensual in

Aesthetics," *Journal of Aesthetics and Art Criticism* 23, no. 2 (winter 1964): 185–92.

11. Merleau-Ponty likens the body in this sense to a work of art. Maurice Merleau-Ponty, *The Phenomenology of Perception* (New York: Routledge and Kegan Paul, 1962), 150–51; also 119n.

12. David Hume, *Inquiry Concerning the Principles of Morals* (New York: Hafner, 1948), 207.

13. John Dewey, *Art as Experience* (New York: Minton, Balch, 1934), 197, 256.

14. William C. Seitz, *The Responsive Eye* (New York: Museum of Modern Art, 1965), 43.

15. Erwin Panofsky, "Style and Medium in the Moving Pictures," *Critique* 1, no. 3; a classic essay, often anthologized.

16. Percival Goodman and Paul Goodman, *Communitas* (New York: Vintage, 1960), 19–21.

CHAPTER SIX
Environment and the Body

1. Quoted in *Waterwalker*, a film by Bill Mason (National Film Board of Canada, 1964).

2. Georgina Tobac, quoted in Thomas R. Berger, *Northern Frontier, Northern Homeland: The Report of the Mackenzie Valley Pipeline Inquiry*, vol. 1 (Ottawa: Ministry of Supply and Services Canada, 1977), as cited in J. T. Stevenson, "Aboriginal Land Right in Northern Canada," in *Contemporary Moral Issues*, ed. Wesley Cragg (Toronto: McGraw-Hill Ryerson, 1987), 387.

3. "Animals, plants, and assorted other natural things and phenomena [are] persons with whom it [is] possible to enter into complex social intercourse." J. Baird Callicott, "American Indian Land Wisdom? Sorting Out the Issues," in *In Defense of the Land Ethic: Essays in Environmental Philosophy* (Albany: State University of New York Press, 1989), 209. This and the following beliefs are based on research among the Ojibwa, but they are common in Native American cultures.

4. Callicott, "American Indian Land Wisdom," 214–15. This and previous quotations are also cited in Dennis McPherson and Douglas Rabb, "Is There Native Philosophy?" a paper delivered at the annual conference of the Society for the Advancement of American Philosophy, Bentley College, Waltham, MA, March 3, 1995.

5. Hin-ma-too-yah-lat-kekht (Thunder Traveling to Loftier

Mountain Heights or Chief Joseph) of the Nez Perce Indians, in Helen Addison Howard, *War Chief Joseph* (Caldwell, ID: Caxton Printers, 1941), 84. Also quoted in T. C. McLuhan, ed., *Touch the Earth* (New York: Simon and Schuster, 1971), 54.

6. Sitting Bull (Tatanka Yotanka), Sioux chief of the Hinkpapa Teton group, quoted in Frederick Turner, ed., *The Portable North American Indian Reader* (New York: Penguin Books, 1974), 255.

7. "For dust thou art, and unto dust shalt thou return." Genesis 3:19. Few poets have expressed the identity of people with place as Wallace Stevens did in "Anecdote of Men by the Thousand" (see note 23).

8. Two accounts that expose this kind of thinking are Susan Griffin, *Woman and Nature: The Roaring Inside Her* (New York: Harper and Row, 1978); and Carolyn Merchant, *The Death of Nature: Women, Ecology and the Scientific Revolution* (San Francisco: Harper and Row, 1983).

9. Maurice Merleau-Ponty, *The Visible and the Invisible* (Evanston IL: Northwestern University Press, 1968), 250–51.

10. Ibid., 250–51.

11. Merleau-Ponty goes to ingenious lengths to overcome the separation of self and world. "The *touching itself, seeing itself* of the body is itself to be understood in terms of what we said of the seeing and the visible, the touching and the touchable. I.e. it is not an act, it is a being at (*être à*). To touch *oneself*, to see *oneself*, accordingly, is not to apprehend oneself as an object, it is to be open to oneself, destined to oneself (narcissism)." *Visible and Invisible*, 248–49; also 250, 256, 274. See also M. C. Dillon, *Merleau-Ponty's Ontology* (Bloomington: Indiana University Press, 1988), 109, 110.

12. Merleau-Ponty, *Visible and Invisible*, 264.

13. Merleau-Ponty's discussion at times becomes difficult and elusive, groping through the interplay of visible and invisible, the flesh of the world and the flesh of my body, seeing and being seen, perceiving and perceived. *Visible and Invisible*, 248–49.

14. Merleau-Ponty, *Visible and Invisible*, 248–49.

15. Merleau-Ponty continues: "I do not see it according to its exterior envelope; I live in it from the inside; I am immersed in it. After all, the world is all around me, not in front of me." "Eye and Mind," in *The Primacy of Perception*, ed. J. M. Edie (Evanston, IL: Northwestern University Press, 1964), 163, 178.

16. Merleau-Ponty, *Visible and Invisible*, 247; also 148–49. See also the translator's preface, lv–lvi.

17. Ibid., 255.

18. Ibid., 63–64. This seems to be contradicted on pp. 70–71: "For me there is no activity and presence of an other; there is on my part the experience of a passivity and of an alienation which I recognize concern me, because, being nothing, I have to be my situation. In the last analysis, therefore, the relationship remains one between me as nothingness and me as a man, and I do not deal with others, at most I deal with a neutral non-me, with a diffused negation of my nothingness."

19. Ibid., 215.

20. Ibid., 260–62.

21. Ibid., 266.

22. Ibid., 262, 261.

23. Wallace Stevens, "Anecdote of Men by the Thousand," in *Harmonium* (New York: Knopf, 1950), 88–89.

24. James J. Gibson, *The Ecological Approach to Visual Perception* (Boston: Houghton Mifflin, 1979).

25. Chris Shilling, *The Body and Social Theory* (London: Sage, 1993), 1, 3, 5.

26. René Descartes, *Meditations on First Philosophy* (Indianapolis, IN: Bobbs-Merrill, 1960), 60, 25.

27. Shilling, *The Body and Social Theory*, 12; also 130.

28. "Distance came to be created between bodies, and the flesh of humans became a source of embarrassment. Consequently, bodies have increasingly to be managed with reference to social norms of behaviour." Norbert Elias, *The Civilizing Process*, vol. 1, *The History of Manners* (1939; reprint, Oxford: Blackwell, 1978); quoted in Shilling, *The Body and Social Theory*, 167; also 134, 163–64.

29. See Yi-Fu Tuan, *Topophilia, a Study of Environmental Perception, Attitudes and Values* (Englewood Cliffs, NJ: Prentice-Hall, 1974).

30. Adrienne Rich, *What Is Found There: Notebooks on Poetry and Politics* (New York: W. W. Norton, 1993), 13.

31. The Pruitt-Igoe public housing project in St. Louis is certainly the most notorious case of a hostile environment. It bred crime and other social ills, and its unhappy inhabitants wreaked their misery in self-destructive ways on their own dwelling places. The situation became so extreme and incurable that the entire project had to be evacuated and the buildings dynamited into oblivion. The case has been widely discussed.

32. Pablo Neruda, *The Captain's Verses* (1952; reprint, New York: New Directions, 1972), 3.

CHAPTER SEVEN
Architecture and the Aesthetics of Continuity

1. See Paul Oskar Kristeller, "The Modern System of the Arts," in *Renaissance Thought,* rev. and enl. ed., vol. 2 (New York: Harper, 1961), 163–227.

2. See Christopher Alexander, *A Pattern Language* (New York: Oxford University Press, 1977), and *A New Theory of Urban Design* (New York: Oxford University Press, 1987). Other architects who, in different ways, unite the practical and the aesthetic include the contemporaries Frank Gehry, especially his Walt Disney Concert Hall; the New Mexico "ecology" architect Michael Reynolds, who uses recycled materials and solar energy; and the Arkansas architect E. Fay Jones, whose Thorncrown Chapel in Eureka Springs, Arkansas, merges architecture and landscape.

3. Keith Thomas documents this change in attitude in *Man and the Natural World* (New York: Pantheon, 1983).

4. James Marston Fitch, *American Building,* 2d ed., 2 vols. (Boston: Houghton Mifflin, 1966–72), 1.

5. See James Marston Fitch, "The Aesthetics of Function," *Annals of the New York Academy of Sciences,* 128, no. 2 (1965): 706–14.

6. Gaston Bachelard, *The Poetics of Space* (New York: Orion, 1964), xxxiii. Appleton's widely cited prospect-refuge theory of landscape experience illustrates the continuing influence of a dualistic architecture of protection exported to environment. See Jay Appleton, *The Experience of Landscape* (London and New York: Wiley, 1975).

7. Wendell Berry, *The Long-Legged House* (New York: Harcourt, Brace and World, 1969); Barry Lopez, *Arctic Dreams, Imagination and Desire in a Northern Landscape* (New York: Scribner's, 1986), and *Desert Notes* (Kansas City, MO: Andrews and McMeel, 1976); Ivan Doig, *This House of Sky: Landscapes of a Western Mind* (New York and London: Harcourt Brace Jovanovich, 1978).

CHAPTER EIGHT
Education as Aesthetic

1. A. N. Whitehead, *The Aims of Education and Other Essays* (New York: Macmillan, 1929), 18.

2. Ibid., v.

3. Alfred North Whitehead, *Science and the Modern World* (New York:

Mentor Books, 1948), 199. See also John Dewey, *Art as Experience* (New York: Minton, Balch, 1934). C. K. Ogden, I. A. Richards, and James Wood, in *The Foundations of Aesthetics* (London: G. Allen, 1925), defined the experience of beauty as "synaesthesia," which is composed of the two elements of harmony and equilibrium. The latter's ultimate value lies in the belief that it is better to be fully than partially alive.

4. Whitehead, *Aims of Education*, 1.

5. The analysis offered here is developed more fully in my book *The Aesthetic Field, a Phenomenology of Aesthetic Experience* (Springfield, IL: Charles C. Thomas, 1970).

6. John Dewey, "The Postulate of Immediate Empiricism," in *The Influence of Darwin on Philosophy* (New York: Henry Holt, 1910), 227, 228.

7. For a fuller discussion of the reality of art, see Arnold Berleant, *Art and Engagement* (Philadelphia: Temple University Press, 1991), chaps. 8, 9.

8. Maurice Merleau-Ponty, *The Phenomenology of Perception* (London: Humanities Press, 1962), 178, 183.

9. Gaston Bachelard, *The Poetics of Space* (New York: Orion, 1964), 86, 88; also 74–77.

10. See Arnold Berleant, "Aesthetics and the Contemporary Arts," *Journal of Aesthetics and Art Criticism* 29, no. 2 (winter 1970): 155–68.

11. Whitehead, *Science and the Modern World*, 196.

12. An educational aesthetic carries definite pedagogical consequences. One result of recognizing the aesthetic in education might be that the occasions for subject, scholar, student, and teacher to come together would be fewer but more precious. Instead of classroom presentations carrying the main load of teaching and learning, they should be fresh springs at which students drink for the refreshment and renewal of their primary educational substance; other techniques would better achieve a mastery of information and skills. The order forced through discipline would be replaced by an aesthetic order. Instead of rigid patterns of behavior imposed from without, a creative spontaneity would develop that is flexible and self-directed in following the movement of thought, the excitement of new ideas, and the unexpected insight or turn of phrase. In place of lesson plans or formal lectures, in which the sequence of ideas has been settled beforehand, there could be the live and unpredictable interchange of ideas generated by the problem at hand. The routine grind of class meetings could be replaced in part by using various participatory devices controlled by the individual student, from audiotapes, computers, and interactive video terminals to research projects and independent investigations outside

the classroom. A major share of the emphasis would fall on methods that engage perceptual experience, such as field trips, independent research, and internship programs.

<small>CHAPTER NINE</small>
Aesthetics and Community

1. B. F. Skinner, *Beyond Freedom and Dignity* (New York: Bantam, 1984), is a notable example of the first of these.

2. John Dewey, *Human Nature and Conduct* (New York: Modern Library, 1922), 134–39.

3. Erich Fromm, *Man for Himself, an Inquiry into the Psychology of Ethics* (New York: Holt, 1947).

4. Environment thus resembles the order of interrelationships we call an ecosystem. My book *The Aesthetics of Environment* (Philadelphia: Temple University Press, 1992) expands and applies this idea.

5. See William James, *A Pluralistic Universe* (New York: Longmans, Green, 1920), lectures 2 and 9.

6. See Berleant, *The Aesthetics of Environment.*

7. Aristotle, *Nicomachean Ethics*, VIII. 4, 13.

8. John Locke, *Second Treatise of Government* (1689); Friedrich Nietzsche, *The Birth of Tragedy* (1870–71); Edmund Husserl, *Cartesian Meditations* (The Hague: Nijhoff, 1960), Fifth Meditation, and *The Crisis of European Science and Transcendental Phenomenology* (Evanston, IL: Northwestern University Press, 1970).

9. See Arnold Berleant, *The Aesthetic Field, a Phenomenology of Aesthetic Experience* (Springfield, IL: Charles C. Thomas, 1970). See also Arnold Berleant, *Art and Engagement* (Philadelphia: Temple University Press, 1991).

10. Martin Buber, *I and Thou*, 2d ed. (New York: Scribner's, 1958), 6–10.

11. "Environmental aesthetics does not concern buildings and places alone. It deals with the conditions under which people join as participants in an integrated situation. Because of the central place of the human factor, an aesthetics of environment profoundly affects our moral understanding of human relationships and our social ethics. An environmental aesthetics of engagement suggests deep political changes away from hierarchy and its exercise of power and toward community, where people freely engage in mutually fulfilling activities. It implies a humane family order that relinquishes authoritarian control and

encourages cooperation and reciprocity. It leads toward acceptance, friendship, and love that abandon exploitation and possessiveness and promote sharing and mutual empowerment." Berleant, *The Aesthetics of Environment*, 12–13.

Reflections on a Reflection

1. Chang Chung-yuan, *Creativity and Taoism* (New York: Julian Press, 1963), 57.

2. *Oxford English Dictionary*, vol. 2 (Oxford: Clarendon Press, 1933), 1151; *Webster's New World Dictionary*, 2d college ed. (New York: Simon and Schuster, 1982), 332.

3. "The question as to what art is—let me answer it immediately and in the simplest manner: art is *vision* or *intuition*." Benedetto Croce, *Guide to Aesthetics* (1913; reprint, Indianapolis, IN: Bobbs-Merrill, 1965), 8.

4. The brief discussion that follows cannot fully develop a theory of environment. I have tried to do this in *The Aesthetics of Environment* (Philadelphia: Temple University Press, 1992).

5. See Arnold Berleant, *The Aesthetic Field, a Phenomenology of Aesthetic Experience* (Springfield, IL: Charles C. Thomas, 1970), and *Art and Engagement* (Philadelphia: Temple University Press, 1991).

6. Chapters 3 and 4 developed aspects of a negative aesthetic critique of environment that are only mentioned here.

7. So, too, with the other arts:

> He had taken a Chinese drawing of geese from the boudoir, and was copying it, with much skill and vividness.
>
> "But why do you copy it?" she asked. . . . "Why not do something original?"
>
> "I want to know it," he replied. "One gets more of China, copying this picture, than reading all the books."
>
> "And what do you get?" . . .
>
> "I know what centres they live from—what they perceive and feel—the hot, stinging centrality of a goose in the flux of cold water and mud—the curious bitter stinging of a goose's blood, entering their own blood like an inoculation of corruptive fire—fire of the cold-burning mud—the lotus mystery."

D. H. Lawrence, *Women in Love* (Cambridge: Cambridge University Press, 1986), 88–89.

Chapter Eleven
Sacred Environments

1. Seven of the canvases have hard-edged black rectangles on a maroon ground, seven are plum-colored tonal paintings. The prevailing tonality is dark and the contrast of hue extremely subtle.

2. Wallace Stevens, "The Anecdote of the Jar," in *Harmonium* (New York: Knopf, 1950), 21.

3. See the discussion of body and environment in chapter 6.

4. *Webster's Ninth New Collegiate Dictionary* (Springfield, MA: Merriam-Webster, 1986), 939.

Index

Printed in the United States
109587LV00002B/4/A

9 780700 608119